There Goes
the Bride

———

There Goes the Bride

✿✿✿

MAKING UP YOUR MIND, CALLING IT OFF & MOVING ON

RACHEL SAFIER

WITH WENDY ROBERTS, LCSW

JOSSEY-BASS
A Wiley Imprint
www.josseybass.com

Published by Jossey-Bass
A Wiley Imprint
989 Market Street, San Francisco, CA 94103-1741   www.josseybass.com

Jossey-Bass books and products are available through most bookstores. To
contact Jossey-Bass directly call our Customer Care Department within the
U.S. at 800-956-7739, outside the U.S. at 317-572-3986 or fax 317-572-4002.

Jossey-Bass also publishes its books in a variety of electronic formats. Some
content that appears in print may not be available in electronic books.

Excerpt in Chapter One from interview with Beth Monchek-Lugo is used with
permission from Beth Monchek-Lugo.

All of the names and identifying characteristics of the brides and their exes have
been changed. This book is not a substitute for counseling or professional, legal,
or financial advice, and the reader should be aware that Web sites mentioned or
referenced may have changed or disappeared since this book was written.

Library of Congress Cataloging-in-Publication Data

Safier, Rachel, 1969-
   There goes the bride : making up your mind, calling it off, and moving on /
Rachel Safier, with Wendy Roberts.— 1st ed.
      p. cm.
     Includes bibliographical references.
     ISBN 0-7879-6748-3 (alk. paper)
     1. Betrothal—United States—Psychological aspects. I. Roberts, Wendy.
II. Title.
HQ801.S34 2003
392.4—dc21
                                       2002154076

Printed in the United States of America
FIRST EDITION
PB Printing   10 9 8 7 6 5 4 3 2

Contents

To the man I almost married: I hope that you, too, have come through this tough time stronger, happier, and better than you were before. I wish you a very happy life.

Preface

❀ ❀ ❀

What does a woman with a broken engagement look like? Well, there's me. When my fiancé "Mark" (not his real name) pulled the plug, I was a thirty-one-year-old writer in Washington, D.C. Before we decided to take the plunge off the mountaintop, I had never thought I was the marrying type. To me, it was like winning the lottery. Both sounded great, but I was doing just fine without them. I pride myself on my independence, taking long trips abroad, solo. I laugh a lot, love to run, and read voraciously, and I've never had trouble getting boyfriends. When my wedding was called off, I reeled. It was right to break up, and I was relieved. So why the hell did it hurt so much?

I needed the stories of other women who had successfully made it through, to assure me that I would, too. I wanted their suggestions for finding comfort and their help in dealing with the "nitty gritty" issues, like telling people my wedding was off and getting money back from vendors. I looked for a book like this to help me heal, but it didn't exist.

So I decided to write it.

Sixty-two "Almost Brides"—women who, at one point, have gone through a broken engagement—answered my call and generously answered a detailed survey I had prepared. It's my privilege to bring their stories to you, in their own words. I have, however, changed their names and those of their exes. Some of these women called off their weddings; others were on the receiving end of the decision. Some eventually realized they were too young to marry; others had gotten engaged in the first place because of fear they were getting so old that they'd better grab their chance. Some escaped abusive fiancés; others were treated like gold but just didn't feel any passion for their partners. Some of these women are now engaged to marry others, some are married, and some are single. Two, after some time apart, reunited with their ex-fiancés and married them. Their different stories are full of humor and hard-won wisdom. And their journeys back to themselves gave me the strength I was looking for.

Though I didn't know any of the Almost Brides before I started writing, I count these amazing women as my friends. In the year it took me to write this book, they cheered me on as they shared the stories of their wonderful lives since their broken engagements. It has been a great pleasure to hear about their weddings and new houses, their pregnancies and career accomplishments. Most important for my recovery, the Almost Brides shared with me the details of the most traumatic time of their lives.

Michael and Harriet McManus, founders of Marriage Savers, a pro-marriage group based in Washington, D.C., like to tell people, "Better the broken engagement than a tragic divorce." I, and the women who share their stories here, couldn't agree more. And yet, until now, the broken engagement has been a taboo subject.

For years, women like us were spoken of in hushed tones. But canceled weddings are more common than people think. If you've met me, you know that I don't talk about my situation in whispers, and I don't hang my head in shame. I was stopped just the other day by an acquaintance I hadn't seen in the past tumultuous year. He asked, "Weren't you getting married?"

I told him we had called it off, and he said, "Oh, I'm sorry. You seemed like such a lovely couple."

"We were a lovely couple," I told him, smiling, my head held high. "We just weren't right for the long haul, and I'm so happy we realized that before we got married."

A year after the fact, with my heart healed and my mind clear, I'm glad that I had misgivings and didn't expect that marriage would make my problems go away. I—and these Almost Brides from twenty-five states and four countries—are proud to be bushwhacking a path for the women who follow. In a society with such a high divorce rate, a greater acceptance of and visibility for broken engagements is a big part of the solution.

We all came to this point from different places. Whether you are trying to decide if you're suffering from cold feet or something more serious, or you—or your fiancé—have already called off your wedding and you need some comfort and help coping, we're here to help. If you are suffering from cold feet, start with Part I. If your wedding has already been called off, begin at Part II.

I wrote this book for me, and I wrote it for you. *There Goes the Bride* combines my story with the wisdom of my fellow Almost Brides and contributing therapist Wendy Roberts. It's got concrete ideas to get you through this time, as well as a Resources section to help (and amuse) you further.

I'm here for you—we're all here for you. I promise, once you're through the tunnel, the light on the other side is strong and bright.

Remember: your Big Day isn't just your wedding day— it's every day.

Best,
Rachel Safier

Acknowledgments

❀ ❀ ❀

So many people and groups helped me make *There Goes the Bride* a reality. My heartfelt appreciation goes out to:

The Almost Brides, who shared a piece of themselves with me. I am in awe of them.

My agent, Stacey Glick of Jane Dystel Literary Management, who understood the dream and helped make it real.

My editor, Amy Scott, and everyone at Jossey-Bass Publishers, who enthusiastically worked with me to get it just right.

The Knot, for providing the very earliest comfort and a fabulous forum for the engaged.

Patron of the arts SMARTHINKING (www.smarthinking. com), for selflessly providing the space for me to create.

Contributing therapist Wendy Roberts, for her professional input.

Bensonn Anspach and Michael Blake for creating the book's Web site, www.theregoesthebride.com.

Corey Ramsden for traveling tech support.

Deborah Permut for helping me figure it all out.

David Blasband for all his kind assistance.

Professor Rebecca Tushnet of New York University for her invaluable assistance with the legal aspects of engagement ring ownership.

The newlyweds who shared their experiences of premarital counseling.

For their input: Beth Monchek-Lugo; Michael J. McManus and marriagesavers.org.; Diane Fields and Catholic Engaged Encounter; Luke Knutson and PREPARE; Dr. Barbara Markey and FOCCUS, Rabbi Daniel Zemel of Temple Micah in Washington, D.C.; Carl A. Gerson of Capacity Coverage Company of New Jersey; Toni De Lisa; Carol Marino of A Perfect Wedding, Inc.; Cleveland Park Library, Washington, D.C.; Joan Schwartz, author of *Macaroni and Cheese: 52 Recipes from the Simple to the Sublime;* and Keith Dresser.

Abigail Trafford, whose book *Crazy Time* helped me in the early days more than she could know.

The Sunnies, my virtual pep squad.

My family and friends, who get me through the hardest times. I hope I came close to showing my love and respect for you here.

Meet the
Almost Brides

❀ ❀ ❀

Sixty-two women with broken engagements in their past answered the call to be part of *There Goes the Bride*. These amazing women are the soul of this book. Let's get acquainted.

WHO ARE THE ALMOST BRIDES?

I asked my fellow "Almost Brides" to describe themselves. Here's what some of them said:

I consider myself to be a mature, intelligent person. I'm very realistic and moderate on most issues. I try to be nice to people, but I'm not a pushover.

I'm shy about approaching people (especially guys) but very talkative and friendly once I meet them. I've been told that I'm cool and easy to talk to. Generally I can get along with most people, though it takes a while for me to make good friends.

—MATTIE

I am an independent woman. I have always gone against the system. It is very important to me to do things right the first time. I am the kind of person who never gives up on anyone or anything. I have struggled for many years with self-esteem issues. My parents were very sparing with their compliments and generous with their criticism. They thought that was the right way to be. It is how their parents were. It has taken me many years to realize that I am not a failure. I still battle those gremlins from time to time but less and less often.

—ABBY

I am a pretty laid-back person. I get attached pretty quickly and easily, and although I don't think I am completely dependent on a man, I don't know if I am completely independent either. I have some major trust issues in my life having to do with my parents' split-up when I was seventeen.

—DEBBIE

I am a black female. Sometimes I believe that I am very strong-willed. Other times I think that I am too nice. I am an outgoing person, but believe I am better one-on-one; large groups tend to intimidate me. My favorite color is yellow, my passion is reading, and I love my family and friends with a devotion that is strong. I am a Catholic, but my faith is being tested somewhat at this point in time. Consider me practicing, but not very well. I am an attorney, but I am not one of those asshole types who walk around saying I am a lawyer. I don't introduce myself by profession. Pretension annoys me. I am a little afraid of getting married, since I called off the prior wedding. I wonder if I brought some bad karma my way by doing that. I am sure that my fears are unreasonable, but now that I am engaged again and planning a wedding, I find that some bad feelings from round number one have resurrected themselves. However, my fiancé is a great man. I feel confident that he is a better man and a better choice for me than fiancé number one. We have been together almost six years, have bought a house together, and have a child. My life is happy. —JESSICA

I am an emotional person, I take things to heart, and I don't like conflict, or change. —STACEY

I'm a fairly independent, career-oriented person. —HEATHER

First child born into a close family, strong Christian beliefs. My parents are about to celebrate their thirtieth wedding anniversary. Did the sorority thing, was an officer. Made lifelong friends during college (added to the three or four from high school that I still keep up with). Got a job as a financial analyst. —TERI

I'm thirty-three. I was thirty-one at the time of the broken engagement. I'm divorced, which happened prior to my meeting my ex-fiancé. I have a four-year-old son who is amazing and wonderful (no bias here). I work as a communications manager for a nonprofit organization. I went to university and have two degrees. —CLAUDIA

I am a thirty-year-old African American mother of two beautiful children. I am an insurance agent and I am studying to be a nurse. I consider myself to be somewhat attractive, intelligent, and also very sensitive. I have a problem with setting boundaries, and I feel a need to be well liked. These are two things that tend to get me in trouble with my children and in relationships. I don't like conflict and confusion, so I let a lot of things pass that should probably be addressed. Other than that, I have an energetic personality, and most people find me to be a joy. —DIANA

I am a happy person. As a rule I laugh a lot. Everyone tells me that's my best quality—that I'm always laughing. I have a quote hanging on my refrigerator that is kinda my philosophy. It says, "We laugh to survive."

I am optimistic, sometimes to my detriment, and trusting, also sometimes naïvely. —AMY

I'm a thirty-three-year-old pregnant bisexual lawyer. I practice criminal defense law. I'm an Episcopalian, living in New York. I'm very outgoing and social. I have three pets. —ELLY

Shy, stubborn, caring, and understanding. —ANDREA

Oldest child, history of short-lived relationships, low self-esteem. —JENNIFER

I'm extremely intelligent, accomplished, and attractive. I have an enormous capacity for love and attach deeply and completely. —TAMARA

An independent, fun-loving woman. I'm thirty-seven, play the clarinet in an all-adult marching band, and I love football and basketball. Gardening is my passion. I got married eight months ago. It is the first marriage for both of us. Neither of us has kids, but we hope to soon. Home includes three cats and a dog. —DEE DEE

Fun, loving, caring person. I fall in love easily and have learned from all my past relationship issues. Strong-willed and independent. My mother was twenty-five before she got married and always wanted me to be self-sufficient before marrying. She encouraged my three older brothers and myself to finish college and have secure jobs/lives before searching for marriage. She was disgusted by the mothers who "pushed" their daughters to look for their future husband in high school. —AVERY

I was born in 1945 to first-generation Jewish parents. My mother is a control freak, and I had the misfortune of having been born on the chubby side. I was dumped on my whole life for it. By the time I was thirteen, I was convinced that I was worthless, because that's what I was told by my family. I lived on the fringes—watched the other girls have dates and join sororities (that's what we did in high school in the fifties). I got into a sorority only because my mother begged her friend to ask her daughter to pledge me. Get the picture? I also have had attention deficit disorder my whole life—something I just realized recently. I didn't do well in school and had no ambition to attend college. I couldn't wait to start working, because I hated school. My mother enrolled me in a school for medical secretaries, and I met my ex through people I hung out with there.

I am now nearly fifty-six years old. When I was thirty-seven—shortly before my second marriage ended—I started college. In my second semester, right after I moved out of the marital abode into my own apartment back in good old Brooklyn, I took two classes and received two grades of "A," which made me realize that I really had a functioning brain. It took me nearly fifteen years, but in 1998, at the age of fifty-two, I graduated with honors. I raised a daughter on my own. I am blessed with three grandchildren. I am in a loving marriage with a man who would rather jump under the wheels of a speeding bus than hurt me. I know who I am, I am proud of who I am, and I finally love me. —NAOMI

I was a teen mom, with a child at seventeen. I had a lot of dreams and goals but was never able to figure out how to achieve them. I have finally gotten to where I wanted to be. An optimistic person, I always try everything to solve a problem, and quitting is a last resort. —GRETCHEN

I am a person who really does see the best in people, no matter what, and many times it has proven to be [to] my detriment. I am the type of lady (because I *am* a lady) who believes that every person on this planet can become something good if they have the proper support and determination to succeed. —MARCI

I am quite a bubbly, friendly person who on the outside seems quite self-assured and confident. Yet on the inside I have been battling to overcome depression for the last sixteen years. This makes me someone who is very good at hiding her true feelings but someone who is deeply caring. I hide my insecurities well and few people know the true me.　　　—FIONA

Fun loving, intelligent, mature, artistic, creative, responsible, moody.
　　　　　　　　　　　　　　　　　　　　　　　　　　—TRACY

I hate describing myself! No, I think I'm a pretty hard worker, motivated to a certain degree regarding my career and other aspects of my life. I'm a hopeless romantic and love drama (the good kind). I think I am a genuine person with a caring heart.　　　—SAMANTHA

I am a very busy person doing heaps of things at once, and I have to be reminded to slow down. I usually get very tired and run down because I've been involved in too many things. As a child I was quite ill, and I basically started to blossom just when I met my ex. I started getting good friends, looking more attractive, and getting my own interests.　　　—SANDY

WHY DID WE ALMOST MARRY?

When I think about the man I fell in love with, I remember a big, tall, smiling man. Beautiful. Athletic. He seemed to me like someone I could travel the world with. In the days and weeks after the wedding was called off, I questioned every thought I'd ever had. Did I date him for the wrong reasons? Did I fall in love too soon, too hard, blindly? Was there a clue in my attraction that would portend the end?

I asked Almost Brides why they had wanted to date their ex-fiancés:

He seemed extremely intelligent. He was also very passionate about his career (he was in the movie business), and I have always been very drawn to artsy people. He was an interesting person with interesting views on life. Plus he had a great head of curly hair and a nice butt. —KIM

He was very attractive, he was class president, [and] he was on the soccer team, which was the only decent sports team on campus. He was smart and fun, and I was quickly the center of his attention all the time.

—ABBY

He made me laugh. He was, and is, a very funny guy. He made me laugh so hard I cried. And he kept asking me out. It took a few months, but I realized that I really enjoyed being around him, so one day I said yes.

—DANA

We ran in the same group of friends. I'd met him a few times, and all of a sudden, he looked really good to me. He'd had the same girlfriend for several years, and they were on the rocks. Something about that unavailability, but almost availability—coupled with all the soulful glances across parties, bars, and so forth—was irresistible. —ELLY

He was fun, wild, good looking. Showed tremendous potential.

—GRETCHEN

He wouldn't take no for an answer! Quite literally, he wouldn't give up. I felt swept off my feet by his persistence, and to actually be accepted, rather than put down, for who I was was a huge attraction.

—HILARY

He didn't have any ugly characteristics—wife, meanness, stupidity, unattractiveness. Seriously, that was how I saw men then: as a presence or absence of Bad Stuff. —KAREN

He offered me everything that I thought I wanted: compliments, attention—heck he practically worshiped me from the very first day. —MARCI

He was different and I was frightened of going home. (I had lived in London all my life. When I met him, I moved to be with him.) I was running away from what I had left behind. —FIONA

I felt like he would protect me, and he was different from any of the other guys I met. —ANSEL

'Cuz he asked. —JENNIFER

I honestly don't know. He was not my type at all, physically. I do know he had an accent that piqued my interest and made me feel connected to him, because my parents are both English. I was blindly unaware of how many problems that would cause; he was an Irish Catholic from Belfast. Until that summer, I thought England and Ireland were close enough in distance that it would bond us to have "similar backgrounds." I should have listened more to the news, I guess. —GRETCHEN

At first I didn't [want to date him], but then, I had never been in a relationship, and he seemed nice enough. —SUSAN

We just "clicked." It was like those years of hating him were all because we were the same person. —ROBIN

He seemed like he had his act together. He had a job, a car, was being a responsible parent. He was attractive. Most importantly and honestly, I was on the rebound from another relationship and I liked having male attention again. —DEE DEE

It seemed our family life was the same and our goals were on track. —ANDREA

Besides being attracted to him, [I find that] he is very, very intelligent and funny. He made me laugh the first night I met him and never tried what all the other guys always do—to have sex with me. —JILL

I think, at first, I really didn't want to date him. I thought he'd be fun to hang around with but not a relationship kind of guy. I really never expected him to call me, but he did and we really hit it off. —BONNIE

I dated him because he seemed fun and funny. He seemed like he could bring excitement to my life and allow me to enjoy life [beyond] just school and work. —JOAN

I saw him as someone similar to me, who enjoyed being with friends. He was quieter than me and I saw that as a bit of a challenge, maybe.

—DONNA

He seemed so different from other guys—he was so playful and fun. He wasn't like the guys I had been meeting; he didn't seem like he was just out to "get some." He seemed to be genuinely interested in me. He didn't seem preoccupied with the tough guy image. There was an attraction between us. He was not the most attractive man I have ever dated—not even close, but there was something very sexy about him. He was very complimentary. When I was with him, I felt like the most beautiful, intelligent woman living, and I felt as though I would be taken care of.

—SOPHIE

Because he had a job, and he liked to read. He seemed to be pretty sensitive and caring. He took an active interest in me, and that was a first [after] a long line of unsuccessful dates. —DIANA

I wasn't sure I wanted to [date him] at first. But I was so insecure about myself at that time that the flattering feeling compelled me to date him.

—PELLA

He was very nice to me, had a great sense of humor, and he was a "nice Jewish boy." Anything else would have been taboo. —NAOMI

[I wanted to date the first guy I was engaged to] because he was comfortable, like an old blanket. [I wanted to date my second fiancé for a] more superficial reason: he was drop-dead gorgeous. —ELIZABETH

CHANGES

Now that I was solo and feeling around to make sure all my parts were still there and in working order, I started wondering: Had I changed for him? If I had, was it for the better or the worse? I hadn't felt myself changing at the time, but after the breakup I suddenly felt more "me," as if I had changed out of too-tight jeans into snuggly pajama bottoms.

I've since learned more about the difference between healthy changes and unhealthy ones. Healthy changes involve making accommodations (something all relationships require), while unhealthy ones change the very person you are. An example of accommodation is the self-described "neat freak" woman in love with a less tidy man. In a healthy effort at compromise, she agrees to divide up their living space. "This is my space," she says of a room or a portion of one, "and I need to keep it neat to stay comfortable." But when it comes to common space, she learns to accept less than pristine surroundings.

An example of an unhealthy reaction is the woman who drops all her friends or interests and takes on her partner's. Or a woman who becomes submissive, because that's what her partner likes.

Unhealthy changes are rooted in a lack of ego strength or the more commonly used term *sense of self*. A woman without a sense of self is more susceptible to change for the worse.

Adolescents are still developing their identities, so many women find it easier to pour themselves into another person rather than continue the process of growing up (one reason why getting married young often isn't a good idea), but aging doesn't always fix the problem. The lack of identity in adults is a deep-seated issue, and therapy can help. So can being aware of issues you have with ego strength.

It's important to realize that your partner isn't changing you. Even if you appeared to have a strong sense of identity prior to a relationship that changes you drastically, the truth is you probably didn't if you were so quick to get lost in a relationship.

DID WE CHANGE FOR HIM?

I asked Almost Brides if their lives changed when they started dating their exes. Did *they* change? Why?

I stopped working out, and everything I did was centered on pleasing and loving Sanford. He was the one who wasn't going to get away.

I stopped loving myself and just put all of my energy into loving him.

I changed because I thought he would never leave if I gave him everything he wanted and even things I thought he might have wanted.

—DIANA

He became my focus over family.

[Being with him caused] lower self-esteem.

[I changed because he] told me I was stupid a lot.

—JENNIFER

My life changed for the better. I went out more often; I started participating more in my life.

I became more motivated. For the first time ever, I thought about going back to college (after twelve years). I began to seek more challenge at work; I basically snapped out of my depression.

He's a very driven person and that was motivating to me. Also, he was the first person [in a while] with whom I really had fun and enjoyed spending time—and that obviously made me much happier and more fun to be around.

—AMY

At first I thought I had found all I was looking for—someone who wouldn't use me and leave me. I got pregnant early on and he stayed. I thought that meant we would make it.

I had to grow up pretty fast, and I became selfless—everything I did had to benefit him or us as a couple. I lost who I was and the ability to see my own needs as something to work for.

[I changed for] two reasons: I was about to become a mother and I was terrified he would leave me alone.

—GRETCHEN

I wanted to be with him all the time. I fell in love too fast. It was my first long-term relationship [and] I gave up all my friends for him. I let my friendships suffer.

—DAWN

This was my first experience with getting involved with a man's family so much so that I felt like I "broke up" with everyone—mom, dad, sisters—and not just him.

Right after I met him, I lost my job. He filled a void. I spent most of my time over at his house. I eventually became a mother figure to his children, as he had custody. I had little time to pursue my goals.

I suppressed my true self. I really didn't want kids at that point in my life and really didn't want to have stepchildren. I was very into a healthful lifestyle and overlooked his smoking and marijuana use. He told me he would stop smoking marijuana after we were married, and I believed him. At some point, he became verbally abusive, and I bought his manipulations. I became weak.

I had made a commitment to him, and I was willing to overlook all the things that were really important to me so that I could honor the commitment I had made.

—DEE DEE

We became very focused on each other. It happened gradually over time. I became really aware of it when he began to tell me [not to] be friends with certain people and to cultivate a friendship with others. Once he told me I shouldn't be friends with my best friend from high school.

I became less independent at first. I desired making him happy. Eventually his domination of my life wore me out and I began to refuse to be ordered around.

I changed because I wanted us to be happy, and it seemed like the right thing to do.

—ABBY

We had a whirlwind courtship. All of a sudden he was staying with me whenever he wasn't working; we were making plans for the future, and the future was suddenly no longer certain [because of the possibility that I had inherited Huntington's Disease from my mother].

I didn't exactly change when we met, although his honesty about life helped promote my own. And his very conservative views helped to mellow out my own liberal ideology. It is difficult, if not impossible, to judge whether or not I changed, because I assumed certain values as my own— values that may not have yet been solidified.

I think most of the change was for the good, in that he helped me to open up a bit.

—HILARY

Our circles of friends were different, so I stopped hanging out with my old friends. I became less involved in my hobbies. I became isolated from most of my friends and lost touch with almost all of them. I had my relationship with him and that was about it. The relationship was new and I was in love. It was my first serious relationship.

Somewhere along the way, I lost my ability to have fun. I got into a rut and lost my passion for my hobbies. I.became ultra serious and conservative—sort of a prude, now that I think about it. I didn't like myself but I didn't know why. He put pressure on me to not go away to school and to stay local, and I guess I let him.

At first I was happy with him. I didn't mind spending so much time away from my friends. I thought they were always going to be there when I was ready to start hanging out again. At first I wanted to spend all my time with him. Then it became a habit. The things that were in my life before were slipping away, but I was too blind to realize it at the time. Looking back, I am surprised that I let him pressure me into not going away to school. I had wanted to do that for so long. I guess I was just blinded by love.   —ERIN

I didn't change a whole lot as a person, though he did help me grow up and lose a lot of that naïveté, and my sense of humor became a lot more sarcastic.

Most of [the change] just came with growing up, though being with him helped shape that (mostly for the better). He has a very sarcastic sense of humor, so I developed one, too.   —MATTIE

I stopped going out so much, stopped meeting new people, started getting better grades. I actually started drinking a little more, because he took pride in drinking a lot of beer.

I became much less social, less outgoing. I made almost no friends in the remaining three and half years of college.

I changed because he was somewhat of a loner/antiestablishment type. I wanted to please him and he wanted to spend all his time with me. I liked that to a certain extent—feeling special and wanted. I always pictured my true love as someone I shared everything with, did everything with, and that's what he wanted, too.   —MELISSA

When I met him, I didn't want to go home. He was my way out, my savior. I didn't gain anything really; in fact, I lost. I come from a lovely home, and he lived in a one-down-two-up filled with damp and mold. At the time, I didn't care how my life was affected. The only good thing at the time was I gained a stepson who was only seven years younger than me, so I could relate to him really well.

I just stopped caring about me in the physical sense. I stopped caring about the way I looked, the way I dressed, and generally took less of an interest in myself.

His life was so different from mine, our backgrounds at opposite ends of a spectrum. I changed to fit in with his life.　　　　—FIONA

We met at school in the fourth mini-semester of my sophomore year of school. Our relationship evolved almost overnight and we began to spend all our time together. I saw less and less of my friends and family to spend time with my ex.

I became less independent and I was always with the ex. I began to hate to be alone. I stopped seeing all my friends, and I only saw the ex.

I changed because I *thought* that was what the ex wanted and I *thought* I had to make him happy. He was very jealous and did not like me being with anyone else.　　　　—ANSEL

I became more comfortable with who I am. That's the perfect way to say it. He made me more confident with my personality and with myself in general. I will always thank him for that.

I feel there is nothing I can't do.

It's hard to say [why I changed]. Maybe [it's] because he's always been so supportive in all of my decisions, no matter how hard they were for me to go through.　　　　—JILL

At first, I didn't change at all, but as the months passed, I found myself quitting activities that I loved because he didn't seem interested in them. My relationship with my family became distant; my sisters and I grew apart. I distanced myself from the very few female friends I had and associated almost exclusively with men.

My self-esteem became closely tied with my ex's approval of my ideas/hobbies/friendships. He never forcibly made it this way—it just evolved that way. I quit activities that I loved because he showed no interest in them, and therefore I thought that they weren't very worthy hobbies. He was not close at all to his family and really wanted nothing to do with mine, so I ended up spending less time with my family. Overall, I started to become very depressed (this is in hindsight; I didn't realize it at the time). I became less trusting of women; I was afraid to let him have a night out alone without me, and [I] became extremely paranoid. I also began to hate my body because he made it clear to me that he preferred the waif look (which I am not even close to being), so I exercised incessantly and basically stopped eating for a while.

Here's the down and dirty on this relationship. His name was Vincent. He never hit me; he never yelled at me. But this was an abusive relationship. I had been out of a relationship for two years when he and I met, and I hadn't dated much prior to that relationship. I guess I really didn't know much about relationships at all when Vincent and I met. He knew how to push my buttons and make me feel like I was less of a person whenever I put "unreasonable" demands on him—little things like asking him to not kiss his ex-girlfriend on the lips in front of me. "No honey, I swear it's just a friendly thing that we do. Don't be so insecure." Yeah, right. Eventually, I broke off all contact with female friends that I had because I thought that Vincent would hit on them. It didn't occur to me that he was the one that I should have broken contact with. He toyed with women's feelings and saw relationships as a big game. I got sucked into that— I thought I'd be a failure if I didn't make him love me.   —KIM

HOW DID WE GET ENGAGED?

After my engagement went belly up, I came up with a theory: the marriages that would go the distance were those that started out with humdrum engagements. To be fair, Mark had gone all out because he thought I'd like a good story to tell others. But now that I thought about it, so many of the happy marriages around me had started inauspiciously over romantic dinners or, in the case of my happily married parents, in my mother's living room (at least according to my father; my mother doesn't even remember it).

Mark had delivered a letter and cash to my office, launching me on an hours-long treasure hunt through the city, with stops at many of the places with special meaning for us (with some extra ice cream joints thrown in; apparently, ice cream was of utmost importance to him). I had been lying prone under my desk with a killer migraine when my boss came in and handed me the envelope with my first clue, but I set out, nonetheless, not wanting to ruin Mark's fun. And I thoroughly enjoyed myself, tipping taxi cab drivers generously, picking up clues from bartenders and ticket concessionaires and ice cream vendors, thickly thinking, I'm getting engaged today, through a haze of migraine medication.

I met up with Mark in a sculpture garden at sundown, and, in a scene out of a chick flick, he kneeled on the ground, looked up into my eyes and, proffering a blue velvet ring box, told me he wanted to spend the next hundred years with me. My mind was a blur. I, who hadn't wanted a ring, and certainly hadn't wanted a man down on his knees, was crying. All I remember thinking was that the ring looked small. (It wasn't. And why did I suddenly care?)

When I polled other Almost Brides, I found that the circumstances ran the gamut. So much for *that* theory . . .

An interesting observation: like me, many Almost Brides described feeling a sort of out-of-body experience. Outside, they were screaming, "Yes!" and inside they were thinking, in the words of Almost Bride Jessica, "This was not how it was supposed to be."

In an out-of-body experience, or, as therapists call it, a dissociative reaction, it's as if we split off from ourselves. The inner person realizes that something isn't right, while the outside person—who wants to be married—gets all excited. This is a red flag. Getting engaged brings up all sorts of emotions, but you should pay attention to any feelings of dread or numbness—or just plain *wrongness*.

I asked Almost Brides to describe such feelings:

[When I accepted the proposal of my second fiancé,] although my lips were saying yes, I just *knew* in my heart there was *no way* I would ever marry this man. —NATALIE

I remember feeling nothing. —SUSAN

I cannot remember my exact words, but somehow I accepted. [I felt] like I had been run over by a truck. Looking back, I think I had hoped [that] if I kept telling him I wanted to wait, then the day would never come. . . . I think I accepted out of guilt more than anything. —ERIN

I was happy and excited but surprised that I wasn't more filled with emotion than I was. . . . I was very surprised at how calm I was. I was a little disappointed with the proposal. I'd had it planned out in Rogers and Hammerstein style for years in my head, and "Will you be my wife?" just didn't cut the mustard. —JODI

Almost Bride Lucy didn't have an out-of-body experience, but her thoughts should have caused some:

[He asked and I thought,] Whoo-hoo! I get to have a wedding!

Curious about their stories, I asked Almost Brides to describe their proposals:

We had been shopping for a few months before we found a ring we liked. I thought it would be some time before we actually got engaged. And one day he came home with a dozen roses for me (it's nothing out of the ordinary for him to surprise me with flowers), and in the middle of the bouquet was a ring box (the kind that looks like a rose). Once he knew that I had seen the box and knew what it was, he said, with tears flowing down his face, "Marry me?" I said yes, of course. I was really excited—and totally shocked and surprised. I didn't think we were going to be engaged officially for at least another eight to twelve months. Immediately after, we sat on the couch and he put the ring on [my finger]. We savored the moment for a while and then called all of our family out of the area—and anyone close by we called [and told] them to stop by.　　　　　—DEBBIE

We had been looking at rings casually for a few weeks and had been to the mall earlier that day. When I was making dinner, he left to run errands and came back with the ring. He gave me a package as I was cooking, which was the ring, and before he said anything, I asked, "Are you crazy?" Then he asked if I would marry him.

I said yes, of course, but told him I didn't expect it so soon. I was under the impression that we were waiting a bit longer.　　　　　—DONNA

He asked me after someone close to me had died, and I remember thinking the ring was a perfect symbol for how life goes on, a circle. I said yes; I was thrilled.　　　　　—ZOË

It was not good. I was in a bad mood all day that day and we had to go to this dinner function for his work. I proceeded to have a few too many drinks, and on the way home, I asked him to drop me off at my apartment. He asked me to come with him to his apartment so he could change clothes, [and] then we'd go to my apartment. I was not very happy with this but went along. When we got there, he went to his room to change clothes and asked me to get him a Coke out of the fridge. I am bitching the whole way to the fridge—Why can't you get your own freaking Coke?—[I] open the fridge and the ring box was sitting on top of the can of Coke. *(Ugh.)*

I took the ring box into his room with the Coke and said, "What is this?" He gets down on one knee and asks me to marry him. I'm buzzing and clearly in a bad mood and the man asks me to marry him. Well, then I felt like crap that he'd been planning this and I am being a bitch, but I said yes, I would marry him. I felt very freaked out. It was pretty surreal. I was obviously flattered that he wanted me to marry him, [and] the ring was absolutely gorgeous, so that was very exciting. I was just very confused.

—AMY

We were eating dinner one night and I asked him if he was ever going to marry me. We had just gone to a wedding two days prior. He actually shocked me and said, "Do you want to set a date?"   —DAWN

I got laid off in October and was basically living with him at the time, and he came in one night all upset about work and told me to get all of my stuff and get out of the house now because he was not happy with our situation. I got very angry and told him that if I left this time and he really did this to me again (especially since I didn't have a job), I would not come back without a compelling reason to do so. I got all of my stuff and really meant what I said.

I put out job feelers, I went home for a week, and I was ready to move on with my life. Well, wouldn't you know it? His week and a half goes by (within two weeks, he would always come crawling back with apologies and I love you's, as well as promises that he would never do this again) and he suddenly has the ring.

He gave it to me in his kitchen as we were leaving to go to dinner. I honestly didn't even realize I was being proposed to. He pretty much just told me that part of my Christmas present was on the shelf, and there was the box. I opened it and looked at it, then sat down and looked at him. He stood there and talked about the ring nonstop. Did I like the cut, is it what I wanted? He picked it out himself, though he wanted to buy me something bigger, and so on. After a few minutes, he asked me why I wasn't wearing it, and I reminded him that he was supposed to ask me something first. He mumbled, "Will you marry me?" [and] then told me that we'd have to keep it top secret until I met his parents because he didn't want them to know before they met me. I agreed to this but said, "only six weeks of secrecy, [and] then it's getting out." —CHRISTINE

I was lying in bed with a nasty headache, and he was sitting at the foot of the bed, twirling the ring on his finger. I asked him what was up, and he asked if I would mind being his wife. It was really anticlimactic, in a way. I was excited that he had finally asked but a little disappointed that it was so informal and unromantic. He didn't even turn the lights on or anything. We made love. —MARCI

We were talking on-line, which was rather appropriate, considering we [had] met on-line as well. . . . [B]oth of us felt like our lives were on hold . . . . I said I had an idea for something that I thought would make us feel better—give us something to work toward, and that, if he wanted, we could keep it between ourselves. He asked what that was and I said, "Marry me." He immediately said, "Yes." I asked him if he [was] sure, and he again said, "Yes." —CLAUDIA

He and I had gotten into our first fight ever and it was a big one. He accused me of cheating, which was completely unfounded. In any case, we spent about three days not talking to one another, and to "make up" for the fight, he proposed. I remember that he got down on his knee, and [I] had this sinking feeling because I knew what he was going to do and I knew

I was going to have to say no. I didn't want to get engaged just because we had had a fight and he felt guilty. So I did say no and he was very upset and cried nearly all night about it. Finally, I told him I would take the ring and think about it.

Here is the part I regret: as I thought about it, I realized that although I wasn't sure I wanted to marry him, I knew I would lose him if I said no and I knew I didn't want that to happen. So, foolishly, three days later, I proposed to him at his parents' anniversary party. —DANA

Number one basically tossed the ring in my lap—I had to put it on myself, and number two went all out and proposed in front of my whole office at our Christmas party on my birthday. In the first case, I remember not wanting to wear the ring but [feeling that] I had to. In the second, I cried and cried. After the first, we sat and watched TV. After the second, we went to a motel. —ELIZABETH

It's hard to say if there was an actual proposal. Somewhere in the three years we dated, I decided to go to law school. When I announced that to him, he got mad at me. I asked him why in the world he'd be mad that I was going to law school. He said that it was impossible for us to do future planning, like buying a house, getting married, and so forth. I was shocked at his mention of marriage; I didn't think that his head was anywhere near that yet. I asked him if he intended [to marry] me. He said, "Well, we've been going out long enough, so yeah." I asked him when he wanted to get married, and he said the next summer. I told him that we could still get married with me in law school, and the summer after my first year would be perfect. He said that might be a good idea. I asked if I should start planning a wedding, and he said, "Sure." That was it. I was very excited. I couldn't wait to plan the wedding. I felt like I had finally won—that he loved me and wanted to spend the rest of his life with me. —KIM

He was such a manipulator and faker! We went to the store and I bought my own ring (warning sign there), and he asked me to wear it to a party we were attending. It was his company Christmas party, and the company stands up to congratulate us and propose a toast. I was so embarrassed! Then he takes the ring back and we go to my parents' house for Christmas. He puts the ring in my stocking, and as we open presents, there it is. He had asked my dad for permission. He had this whole hokey speech ready, and [then] he asked me. I felt so conflicted. This was not how it was supposed to be.

—JESSICA

At the time Sanford proposed to me, our relationship was on hiatus because I wanted something more from the time we had spent together. I made radical changes in the way I look and the way I spent my spare time. We had never lived together and he had accumulated a wardrobe at my house. I gathered the clothes and took them to him. I started going out with my friends on the weekend. One day, when I was coming over to pick up my daughter from a visit, he took me into the bedroom and said, "I want to stop playing games with you. I don't want to be with anyone else and I think we should get married. I am going to try to save up $5,000. Can we go to Vegas and get married?" I was stunned. I asked him where we were going to live, and he said in the home that I had purchased. I was like, "Oh." Then I asked him if he was sure that this [was] what he wanted. He said yes, so I said yes. I was happy and relieved. I felt like everything was going to be fine and I would have his love and support in raising our children.

—DIANA

We were engaged [after] one month [of] dating, but we were very young and we did not tell anybody. Later, when I was nineteen and he was twenty, we were engaged for real.

The first time, we were on my back porch at my parents' house. He got down on one knee and asked me to be his wife, with a twenty-five-cent ring out of a bubble gum machine. The second time, he took me out to dinner and out for a drive. We got back to my parents' house and I went into the bathroom. When I came out, he was on one knee in front of the bathroom door. He said he could not imagine his life without me and asked me to be his wife. We had an engagement ring made from some of my family diamonds.

The first time, I felt excited and happy. The second time, I felt a big letdown and was not excited at all. It just felt like something that had to happen.　　　　　　　　　　　　　　　　　　　　　　　　　—ANSEL

It was Valentine's Day. We were at my apartment. I was unemployed, so I had a lot of time to make dinner and get myself all dressed up. He brought flowers, we had a drink, [and] then he pulled out a ring and simply said, "Will you marry me?" I felt some dread, then some excitement. I said yes. [I felt] some dread because after the initial bringing up of the subject of marriage, and even after looking at rings, I decided this was *too soon*. I barely knew this man. I specifically told him *not* to propose, especially on Valentine's Day. He did it anyway. I thought that since he had gone against my wishes, he must really love me to risk that kind of rejection. (Ha!) So I said yes, but I did feel some pressure, too. The thought of a *wedding* was exciting to me.　　　　　　　　　　　　　　　　　　　　—DEE DEE

I was shopping with my mother, and Matt kept calling my cell phone—he was anxious for me to come home soon. When I finally did, he was standing in the hallway looking strange. I thought, I wonder if he's about to propose. He asked me [to] step outside with him. We sat down and [he] told me how he loved me and how wonderful I had been to his family (who was visiting that weekend). Then he got down on one knee and asked. I told him he better not be joking. He said he wasn't, and I said, "Yes."

It felt strangely unimportant—like it wasn't happening to me.

　　　　　　　　　　　　　　　　　　　　　　　　　—CAROLYN

One night, he brought me home from one of our dates and said, "If you lose twenty pounds I might just ask you to marry me." Next day I was on a starvation diet. Actually, he never did propose formally. He told me he was having the ring made (his mother had the center stone and my mother had some small diamonds; he had them made into a pear-shaped cluster ring), and he brought it over one night.

That was kind of all there was to it. I was totally blown away. I felt special—wanted. —NAOMI

We had never talked about marriage. He was in the process of getting a divorce, and we had only been together about three months! He bought a ring and I had *no* idea. I was babysitting, and he had gone to the mall and bought me some presents. He felt an "urge" to go into the jewelry store and spontaneously bought the ring. He wasn't going to give it to me till after Easter (he was coming home to meet my parents), but [he] was like a kid in a candy store. He gave me the presents of clothes and couldn't wait any longer. I was looking at a sweatshirt, and he got down on one knee and proposed. Not my dream place, but he was *so* happy! All he said was, "Will you marry me?" (and that he [had] wanted to ask me in a special way, but he just loved me so much, he couldn't wait to ask me). I said yes. I felt shock, surprise, joy. I loved him, too, very, very much and hated when he had to leave to go back to his army post.

—AVERY

He asked me on *his* birthday—after a romantic dinner, on his knee. He said the appropriate sappy things. Even though I was thinking of leaving him, he asked, so I thought, of course, I'll say yes. —JENNIFER

I think we just both kind of decided. I don't remember any formal proposal. I was nervous, unsure of whether I wanted to, but even more unsure of whether anyone would ever ask again. —PELLA

Nothing romantic. We talked about it, [and] looked at rings, and once we had a ring, I just wore it. I remember thinking that it wasn't how I thought it would be. No hearts, flowers, or chocolates. But I still thought, Why not? He loves me, so it must be okay. —FIONA

We were eating brunch at a restaurant. I had pretty much made it clear he needed to propose to me, so he did. Not very romantic. No ring. Of course, I said yes. Since I'd practically ordered him to propose.   —ELLY

After six years of being together, he had to know whether he was going to marry me or not, so I told him he had six months to decide, and after six months, if he didn't propose with a ring, I was going to start seeing other people. I told him that it was not an ultimatum and that I still wanted to be with him, but I needed to get on with my life already! Apparently, the thought of me dating other people was too much for him, so he proposed on the very last day of the six months.

It was extremely *un*romantic. He waited until the very last second to go and buy the ring. It wasn't even an actual ring; it was a loose diamond in a temporary band. He went to the jeweler that morning and bought it. When he came back, I knew where he had been. We sat down in his living room, and I knew what he was about to do and I started giggling! He got down on both knees and just said, "Will you marry me?" I said, "Yes" through my laughing. He had to take the diamond back to the jeweler to set in an actual band, so I didn't even get the ring for another week or so. I felt relieved. I felt like I had paid my dues for so long and I was finally getting my payoff. I was excited. I wanted to start planning the wedding that moment.   —SOPHIE

We were spending Fourth of July weekend at [our] friends' cabin, with [our] friends and another person. Basking in the sun on our porch, alone together, he pulled out the ring and said, "Will you marry me?" Interestingly, I knew he had the ring—I'd "approved" it before we left, but I didn't think he'd propose so soon afterwards. (He knew I wanted a set-up, nifty scenario instead of a casual question.)

I said, "I have always wanted to marry you." Weird, huh?

—KAREN

He had been joking about it for a week and officially asked the words one night while we were in bed. There was no planned proposal or huge event. He just blurted out, "Will you marry me?" I said, "I guess so." I specifically remember thinking I wasn't ready but that I couldn't bring myself to tell him. He was so excited, and I didn't want to hurt his feelings. I figured this wasn't a *real* proposal, since he didn't have a ring. I figured I could go with the flow and that we would realize in time if things weren't going to work out. —HILARY

It was after school in the vestibule. He got down on one knee and asked me to marry him. I said, "Yes, now please get up." I felt embarrassed. First thing we did was figure out how to hide the ring. —DANIELLE

It was New Year's Eve. We were celebrating alone at home, dancing in our living room to a slow song. He told me [that] at the end of the new year he wanted me to be his wife. I was still eighteen and dreamy-eyed. I said yes, and I loved him *so much!* I felt like I was the most special girl in the world and all my dreams were about to come true. —GRETCHEN

I used to bartend, so I worked incredibly late hours, usually getting home every night around 4 to 6 A.M. I had worked six days straight with this schedule and would sleep all day. One Saturday morning, he was being very noisy. I woke up, sat in bed for about an hour, and started getting angry at him for being inconsiderate, [thinking about] how he *never* cleans and that I just didn't have the energy to do so. I woke up bitching at him and just basically said, "Screw it," and went back to bed. He came up and apologized and brought out the ring. It was a weird proposal but appropriate for the relationship. —JILL

We were driving home to his parents' house and the ring was in the glove compartment. Nothing too eventful. I didn't say anything. I was shocked because I did not think he was going to do it. —LAURA

It was 7 A.M., I was sound asleep, and he woke me up. He said he had been up all night watching me sleep, thinking about how much he loved me and how he didn't want to live without me; he wanted to be there to protect me from any harm. So he had me sit on the side of the bed, got down on one knee, and said, "I love you with everything that I have in me. I can't imagine my life without you. Will you marry me?" Well, obviously, through tears, I said "Yes!" I felt this overwhelming sense of joy. It was the happiest moment of my life.

—STACEY

We took a Fourth of July trip to Chicago. We both like baseball, so he surprised me with a day trip to Dyersville, Iowa, where [we visited] the field [that had been filmed for] the movie *Field of Dreams*. In front of about thirty people (strangers), on home plate, he got on [one] knee and asked. He had cornered some poor lady earlier and asked her to take pictures of the whole thing.

I specifically remember a fleeting thought: *oh no, we're in public; I can't say no!* And then [I said to myself], "You're just shocked. You're really okay with this."

—TERI

With the help of these Almost Brides and therapist Wendy Roberts, let's figure out whether you're suffering from cold feet or something more serious.

Part 1

MAKING UP YOUR MIND

Is This Just Cold Feet?

❁ ❁ ❁

I *knew* that I was doing the right thing, that I was with the right guy and I was only *nervous* about the *wedding*. Well, that nervousness manifested itself in ways that should have been warning signs to me. I would wake from a dead sleep in a sweat, panicked about the wedding. When I would daydream about our upcoming life together, I would get panic attacks and think, I can't go through with this! I excused those feelings as my being nervous about standing up in front of everyone at the wedding. That's pretty uncharacteristic of me; I have never been the shy type and have never been afraid of public speaking or being the center of attention. I remember thinking, I'm not even sure that he's going to show up for the wedding; I should call it off now. When I would voice my concerns and fears to him, he would reassure me, telling me that I was being irrational. Doesn't seem that way anymore!

The good that has come from that aspect of the broken engagement is that I have learned to trust my own instincts. What seemed at the time like cold feet turned out to be more of a genuine and deep-down fear that what I was about to do was not the right thing for me. I think I allowed myself to be so blinded by the wedding and the thought of just having *someone* that I ignored the obvious signs. The thing that made it so hard for me at the time was that he wasn't a "bad" guy; he wasn't abusive and he treated me pretty well. But "it" just wasn't there. We were different enough that a marriage between us would not have worked and I knew it. I just did not want to admit it to myself. We wanted different things out of life, and the differences were drastic enough that it would have caused us to eventually go our separate ways. I'm just thankful it happened *before* the wedding.

—SOPHIE

If you hang out on the chat boards at TheKnot.com or read the e-mails I get from women who visit my Web site, www.theregoesthebride.com, you'd think nearly every bride who ever said yes to a proposal gets cold feet.

And I don't doubt it's true.

Dating is one thing, but signing up for the rest of your life is liable to give anyone a few second thoughts. The challenge is deciding if you're suffering from garden-variety cold feet or what I call "frozen footsies"—a much rarer malady whose only cure is calling off the engagement.

MY STORY

In my case, I thought because I couldn't put into words what was holding me back from wanting to get married, I had no "good" reason not to. My fiancé was (and I'm sure still is) a wonderful, caring person. I loved him. If he felt it important to sign on the dotted line, I really should, right? I didn't want a big wedding, but if he did, I really should, right? (You can't take someone's dream of a big wedding away from him, can you?) But as time went on, I kept doing the same dance. I'd feel one way and he'd be opposed, so I bent farther and farther backward till my back literally ached.

As we got closer and closer to the wedding day, I felt worse and worse. Because I couldn't (or wouldn't) put a name to what I was feeling, because he was wonderful and I loved him, I decided to stick it out. But my body and my mind wouldn't let me. I got migraines, often. I had nightmares, frequent colds, and lost a lot of weight. I was short-tempered and wandered around thinking, "No one knows the way this relationship really is." Even then, I thought I must be wrong. Now I know that the only thing wrong is marrying someone you are not 100 percent committed to.

FACE THE TRUTH

But it's easy to have that knowledge after the fact. At the time, I just kept bending. Instead of saying, "this is what I want" and finding a relationship to fit those parameters, I made myself fit the lines that were already drawn. As Almost Bride Christine says, "I just wanted to make it work. Never again will I do this. I guarantee that!"

Almost Bride Lisa says,

Now that it is over, I can recall a number of times that for a few minutes I would think that the whole thing was a bad idea. Would I love him forever? But I just chose to ignore it and chalk it up to cold feet.

The first step is deciding that if what you're suffering from really is frozen footsies, you'll call off the wedding. Now is the time to face the truth.

The second step is accepting if yours is a nonnegotiable situation. Many problems can be fixed or simply aren't important in a life of imperfect humans trying their hardest. But certain points are iron clad. Listen up:

NONNEGOTIABLES

1. *If your fiancé hurts you,* call it off. There are no second chances when violence is involved. If some aspect of your relationship is scaring you and you need to talk or need help finding safety, you can call the National Coalition Against Domestic Violence hotline (NCADV), twenty-four hours a day, any day, at 800-799-SAFE. Deaf callers can call 800-787-3224 for a

TTY connection. You can also check out their Web site at www.ncadv.com. There is a button to click on the site if you don't want the fact that you visited to register in your computer.

2. *Emotional violence* is harder to spot. If your fiancé disrespects you or has habits, friends, or views that you find disrespectful, speak up. *Respect should be a no-brainer,* and actions including constant criticism are definitely a red flag, but it is possible that your fiancé isn't aware of his hurtful words. It's also important to realize that "endearing" traits like possessiveness can develop into physical violence. If you make yourself and your needs clear and the emotional violence continues, run. The NCADV can help you figure it all out.

3. *How about if it's his mother who's rotten?* Many mothers-in-law are none too pleased about their future daughter-in-law homing in. You'd think moms would be happy to see their sons happy, but that's not the case for many women. As for your situation, Rome wasn't built in a day, and if you're going to call off the wedding because someone in your fiancé's circle is less than enamored of you, well then, do it now. The more important question is: *Does your fiancé stand up for you?* This is part and parcel of point number two. Your marriage has to be the top priority, you have to be a team, and he's got to be a man, or his mother can have her little boy back.

4. *Marriage doesn't fix problems, it only makes them permanent.* If you're going into this in the hopes that signing on the dotted line will make one of you stop cheating, stop finding someone of your own sex more appealing, or generally compel you to clean up your act, you're fooling yourself. As the poet Maya Angelou so wisely said, "When someone shows you who he is, believe him."

5. On the same line of reasoning, *if you're going into this in the hopes that you can change him once it's "legal,"* see point number 4 in this list. If you believe he wants to change you, see number 4. Marriage should be about pledging your future to someone you want to grow old with. *As he is, as you are, forever.* Does that sound too long?

6. *Communication is key.* Ask your mom, talk to your friends, see a therapist. But if you want to tie your future to his, you two must be able to talk about everything. *If you worry about bringing some topics up for fear of his reaction, or if either of you is unable to speak clearly and openly about your wants and needs,* you will have trouble. Marriage isn't dating and it isn't just a friendship. There is no skating over the rough spots.

7. *Wedding planning is stressful.* You have to decide/ feel/know if your trouble is about guest lists and wedding budgets or family problems that will last longer than a day and money problems that can't be rectified. As with every other point on this list, is your fiancé willing to work with you? *Is this a problem that will haunt your marriage?* My ex-fiancé and I had a doozy of a time planning our wedding. We wanted *very* different things: he wanted the full formal affair and I wanted to elope, and, in our case, these differences reflected much more important differences between us.

8. *The wedding is one day.* Some women love the fairy tale, all-eyes-on-me extravaganza (can you tell I don't?). Remember, after the wedding, the couple rides off into the sunset. *Is he the one you want across the breakfast table from you every morning?*

9. If you find yourself saying, *"I love him but . . . ,"* smack yourself. Those are the most frightening four words in the English language. Those words should always be followed by scary horror movie music. They are not only a red flag, they are a tent-sized red flag with fireworks popping around them.

10. If, for whatever reason, *marrying this guy doesn't resonate with you,* doesn't feel wonderful (difficulties in living together or planning a wedding notwithstanding), call it off. *There are cold feet, and there is the deep knowledge in you that this isn't right.* A whole life together is a very long time.

Okay, you might think, none of those leap out at me. Good. Then you're in a mature relationship. Just maybe not the right mature relationship.

IS IT ME OR IS IT HIM?

When trying to figure out if your feet are cold or frozen solid, it's important to decide: Is it me or is it him? Maybe you're worried about losing your independence. Maybe you worry about altering your identity when you go from "Ms." to "Mrs." Maybe you're anxious about sharing a home with someone, every day, and not having a place to retreat to if you fight. Maybe you wonder if you'll even *like* being married. These are all examples of it being you, not him.

If, instead, you're stressing because he's unreliable and you resent it, or he flirts with other women and you get insecure, or he embarrasses you in front of your friends and you're getting to the point where you're cringing whenever he opens his mouth in front of them, the issue is him or, rather, the differences between you and him. I'll get to these interpersonal issues later in the chapter.

For now, let's focus on you. If you're pretty clear that you'd feel anxious even if you were marrying Prince William, you need to do some exploring. Writing down your thoughts and feelings in a journal can often be helpful in clarifying your specific fears and issues. Talking to close friends and relatives about what you are thinking and feeling—as well as listening to what married friends felt when they were engaged—may be reassuring. When I wondered if it was cold feet, women on The Knot recommended I pick up *What No One Tells the Bride* by Marg Stark. It's a great book, but it didn't fill the gnawing hole inside me the way it did for others. That was one clue that my misgivings were more serious.

If none of these pathways brings you real, lasting comfort and you continue to struggle with a chronic uneasiness that doesn't seem to be connected to your fiancé, you might want to consider talking to a therapist.

And if you find it impossible to tell if your anxiety is internal or interpersonal, you could also benefit from speaking to a professional. You may only need a handful of sessions to sort out the specific issues and resolve enough of your anxiety to feel ready to move forward with the marriage. Or you may discover that your anxiety signals a great deal of underlying conflict that needs to be addressed and resolved. If this is the case, I don't need to tell you that it's better to work on yourself *before* getting married. It's much easier to postpone the wedding now than marry with major issues unresolved (and possibly unidentified). Such problems aren't going to magically go away when you say, "I do."

It may help to start with your thoughts on marriage. What does marriage mean to you?

STRONG MARRIAGES, NOT FAIRY TALES

I asked Almost Brides to describe their ideas of marriage before they met their fiancé and after they split up. Many found that their original images were unreasonable. Going through the experience of a broken engagement opened their eyes to the fact that fairy tales don't exist. They shifted their priorities accordingly, putting themselves in a better position to have a stronger marriage down the road.

With hindsight, I realize I had *no idea* what marriage meant when I met my ex. All I had was a "movie" idea of what a wedding was, and by that I mean that I was unable to see much further than that one day, that one event. I thought love was supposed to be like it was in the movies; you meet, fall in love, and get married. I guess I thought I would figure the rest out later.

Those ideas have absolutely changed. I now know that *marriage* is the most important part and the wedding is just a celebration. Marriage is not easy and it's certainly not like it is in the movies! It is work, hard work at times, and both parties must be up for the challenge. One person can never love enough for both of them. —DANA

I thought marriage should make you happy almost all the time, and the two people should be equal and always work together. Being married meant you love[d] this person and stayed with them forever, accepting all flaws with the good stuff. I truly thought any problem should be resolved with a little hard work.

My relationship with my ex never really coincided with these ideas. I thought that would change once we were married.

I've learned a lot about "acceptable flaws" in a person and that sometimes problems won't change. I still believe in unconditional love, but I learned that it has to exist on both sides. And respect for each other, as a partner and an individual with their own ideas, is essential. —GRETCHEN

I honestly don't think I had a clue about marriage either time [I got engaged]. Even though I wasn't young and had been "around the block" a bit, I think I was still looking at marriage as some sort of fairy tale—complete with the white picket fence and, of course, Prince Charming. My parents have been married for forty-three years to each other and are still very much in love. I know that this is what my ideal was, but I really didn't know anything about how to obtain it. I really was extremely naïve when it came to long-term relationships and commitments. I thought they just "happened," like a lightening bolt kind of a thing, and I honestly did not realize how much work and effort goes into those relationships.

Wow, have I ever changed! I have, thanks to both exes, a much better understanding of relationships. . . . I have discovered that true honest love grows from time and effort placed. Of course, sparks and chemistry are present, but for a relationship to be solid, you have to have the ability to communicate honestly and openly without fear. A "true" love will respect you for this, not put you down. —NATALIE

[Before, I thought of marriage as] a partnership that requires a lot of hard work, where the individuals are in it because of the strengths that the other brings to the relationship, not because they "need" each other. The individuals constantly challenge each other to be their best.

Oh, yes, those ideas have changed! My mom gave me the analogy that I continue to use when I talk about relationships: marriage and love are supposed to feel like that big comfy terry cloth bathrobe that you love to put on in the morning. It's not about challenges; it's about warmth, understanding, and acceptance. Both individuals should have similar goals, but the challenge to learn and do new things must come from within, not from another person. —KIM

Honestly, I thought that marriage wouldn't be much different than dating. But then again, as most little girls do, I dreamt of my wedding and I thought my marriage would be just like a fairy tale. I thought Sanford and I would be like Claire and Cliff Huxtable, or Will Smith and Jada. I was twenty-nine years old, I already had two kids, and I didn't want to be a statistic single black woman whose children had different daddies. I wasn't brought up that way and it made my parents look bad. I knew that Sanford and I didn't have a good working relationship, and I didn't care. What was more important to me was to be married. I didn't want to go back to dating and then get to know someone and then find out that [I didn't] like [him], and then meet someone else [, only] to find [that he wasn't] the right one either. Dating can be a vicious cycle, and I figured that with Sanford I knew what the worst would be and I felt I could accept it. I also thought that marriage would help level out all the responsibilities of parenting. So I guess, to me, marriage was going to be the elixir for my troubled life.

Marriage is forever for me, and forever can be a long time, especially if you're unhappy. I also learned that marriage doesn't change people. If a person is irresponsible before you marry him, he will always be that way, unless it is him who changes.

I learned that marriage requires that you and your partner be evenly yoked. This was a term that I never heard of until I planned my wedding and attended counseling with the pastor of the church. [Being] evenly yoked means that both partners share the same commitment in a relationship. If the commitment isn't shared, the marriage will be doomed before it even starts. —DIANA

I have always wanted to get married and have a family. I had idealistic views about marriage until I was engaged and forced to think more about it.

My ideas have completely changed. I have learned that if something doesn't feel right, it probably isn't. I have also learned that for a marriage to work you must have similar values and, most importantly, be able to communicate about everything. I also now want to marry someone that I am emotionally and spiritually connected with. I now feel marriage has a spiritual purpose and is not just a way to have a family.   —LAURA

My idea was that once you had found "the one," you should be committed ASAP! Why wait if he's the one, right? Mind you, I don't mean rushing into marriage (we were going to wait four years), but I guess I rushed into the engagement. I just figured it would keep me more settled, and I wouldn't have to worry about guys and dating anymore. I could focus on school.

Now I realize how much work really goes into a marriage. I just got fed up with the work and broke it off (we were in different states). I realize now that I just didn't love him enough. I would never have given up on my first love or my current husband like that.   —ROBIN

My ideas of marriage were the fairy tale. I would fantasize about the two of us cooking dinner together, raising our children. I assumed that by the ripe old age of thirty I would be married and have toddlers running around my house. I figured I would be a stay-at-home mom. Pretty much the entire "June Cleaver" image minus the pearls. Everything would be peachy most of the time, and any argument we would have would end with kisses and hugs.

That's changed tremendously. I have a far more realistic view of marriage. I know that I probably won't be flitting around the kitchen in a freshly pressed dress when hubby gets home. When the day finally comes around that I do get married, I know there will be disagreements about money and raising children and who left the cap off of the toothpaste. I know that it is a partnership that both people have to contribute to. I know that my life does not stop because I am in a relationship.   —SOPHIE

For other Almost Brides, calling it off only strengthened their original views and their desire to hold out for a strong partnership that would weather the tough times and the years:

My ideas of marriage have been greatly shaped by my Christian upbringing. I believe divorce is a sin in God's eyes and I have always said I would avoid it at all costs and would never go into a marriage thinking, well, if it doesn't work out, I can always get a divorce. My parents are about to celebrate thirty years. My mom's parents are going to hit sixty [years] this month. And my dad's mom is the luckiest woman in the world: my dad's dad ([who] died before I was born) and my grandmother were deeply in love and were married for about thirty years. A few years after he died, she married a man whom she loved and cherished for twenty-four years, until he died this past summer. I know I am extremely lucky in this day and age to have grown up around so many wonderful marriage role models.

I still want everything my parents have. In fact, going through one engagement worked to instill [in me] the importance of being with the right person. I know how much work a marriage will take, and I'm willing to go the distance. —TERI

It is a partnership between two people. And equal as can be. No one has more say than another (this is not the 1950s). But I also feel that strong marriages and relationships are built on trust and faithfulness and communication. To me, these are the most important. And invaluable. I truly believe that without a healthy balance of these, a marriage won't work. I also believe that a healthy balance *can* be achieved. [And be] permanent. Something that is going to last forever. No matter what is going on (well, with the exception of abuse or cheating), it can be worked out. Like I told my fiancé, "I'm not going to take off just because we hit a rough patch—it can't be all roses all the time."

If anything, what happened only solidified my beliefs. —DEBBIE

I think that my ideas of marriage are somewhat skewed because of the rampant divorce rate in my family. My parents divorced when I was nine years old. The thing that I most [thought] of when I considered marriage was that I want[ed] to be in it for life. . . . I don't think I ever had the fairy tale vision of marriage, since I know that it takes work to keep a good relationship going.

I don't think my ideas have changed much. I know now, for a fact, that it takes a lot of work to make a relationship work.   —BONNIE

A partnership for life. Support each other through everything, a shoulder to cry on, and a friend to laugh with. A marriage has to be a friendship also (which is where I think my ex and I went wrong; our friendship was not that strong). I thought of marriage as a union of two people who loved each other and wanted to stick through thick and thin forever.

No, those ideas really haven't changed.   —VALERIE

Like most young people, I think my views of marriage were heavily influenced by my parents' marriage, coupled with modern, forward-thinking ideas of partnership. Before my mother got sick, I believe my parents had a very strong, very loving, and very equal marriage. They were traditional in many ways—my mother stayed home to raise the children while my father worked long hours to be able to afford private school, but as a child I understood them to be partners. I always believed that my husband and I would be, first and foremost, best friends, as well as intimate lovers. But I also expected us to play different roles when it came to raising a family. We may be equal, but we can't both do everything.

I don't believe those ideas have changed.   —HILARY

I always wanted a marriage—just like my parents' but different. My parents are very happy together, but my dad is very much the domineering one, the breadwinner, and so on. In my opinion, they don't talk/share enough, and they have some "balance of power" issues. However, it works for them and it's clear they love each other. I wanted (and still do [want]) a marriage that is truly equal, with shared responsibilities, equal involvement in the children's lives (time as well as money earned to support them), and lots of fun, lots of laughter.

Those ideas haven't really changed, but I realize now that my goals wouldn't have been achieved with my ex. —MELISSA

Before [my] ex, my idea of marriage [was] that people should be respectful and have fun together, as my parents, who have been married for thirty-seven years, do.

My ideas have not changed since then. —KELLY

Still others, like Almost Bride Jill, admit to still figuring out what marriage means to them and if it has a place in their lives:

Before I met him, I never wanted to get married. I thought it was a hassle and not something that fit my personality. I can be pretty selfish emotionally at times and have a hard time giving myself up to someone.

As we got to know each other, and felt comfortable with each other, I trusted him with my heart . . . and still do. I just don't trust my own heart, I guess . . . and [I] am horribly afraid of routine. I see marriage as not really being stuck but as a routine that has been engraved into our society as the norm.

HE SAYS TOMATO, YOU SAY TOMAHTO

If you think that, yes, you do want to be married, and you've got a firm grip on your own issues, it's time to take a look at the uncertainties that stem from basic differences in your personalities. The funny thing is, these differences often have a lot to do with what drew you to him in the first place (after all, opposites attract). They may prove complementary and help you to balance each other out (for example, you may be very organized, but sometimes too rigid and systematic, while he's disorganized, often forgetful, but very spontaneous and fun to be with).

Almost Bride Lisa wanted to marry her fiancé because:

I thought we balanced each other out, because we were sort of opposites. He had things I could take from him, and he could take [things] from me.

But, as you've seen, conflicts can arise out of basic differences in personality and character, so it's important to evaluate both sides of the coin.

For instance, a very driven, intense, goal-directed person may be attracted to a partner who appears to be easygoing and laid-back, but he may actually only appear laid-back; his behavior could really be a defensive maneuver to ward against anxiety resulting from facing the real demands of life. Thus the flip side of his coin may include tendencies toward procrastination, avoidance of responsibility, and the general refusal to take charge of his life (major passivity). If this is the case, the driven, intense, goal-directed person will likely become even more driven and intense and probably anxious and increasingly resentful at the added responsibility she has to take on to compensate for her partner's behavior. And in response to this, he will typically settle back in his passive, procrastinating style even more, knowing that his highly competent, focused, and persistent partner will take care of it all. (And probably, even though it appears that he has the easier road and gets away with a lot, he's likely to feel inadequate and resent the loss of control). The dynamic between them actually intensifies each of their character traits and behaviors and drives them apart.

This is not to say that every wonderful trait of your partner hides a darker side, but, rather, that it's important to keep your eyes open. Before walking down the aisle, you need to make sure you see your partner for who he is. Equally important is knowing what his needs are and that you can meet them.

And, of course, you need to ask yourself what your most basic, important needs are—not what others think they should be, but what really matters to you and what you look for in a mate. Is it important that he is often affectionate and physically demonstrative, helping you feel loved and desired? Do you need him to share his feelings for you to feel close and connected to him? Are you a person who can only feel secure and safe if he's reliably where he said he would be when he said he'd be there? Even if you plan to work on your own issues or insecurities in the future, don't minimize the significance of his behaviors and capacity for intimacy. Don't count on working out all of your insecurities and convince yourself that you will "deal with it" when it comes to his.

THE APPLE DOESN'T FALL FAR FROM THE TREE

Be sure to also give weight to any concerns and anxieties you have about his family as well as values and background differences—including religious, cultural, ethnic, and socioeconomic differences. It's not that two people need to be replicas of each other for a successful marriage to happen; rather, you both need to be realistic about the impact of significant areas of difference so you can evaluate the chances that these issues will become major dividing forces.

Look closely at the parents of your fiancé, because they may very well serve as a forecast of how your partner will develop over time. This can be true even if he seems to reject or dislike certain traits or behaviors. I read a marriage test somewhere once and a question resonated with me: "If your fiancé becomes more like his parents as he ages, would this be okay?"

GUT FEELINGS

Finally, going back to the Nonnegotiables, don't ignore any nagging but vague uneasiness you have about your relationship. Sometimes people can acknowledge that something doesn't quite feel right, even if they can't really articulate what it is. Instincts can be the most important indicator of all. So it's important to pay attention to them—they can reflect an unconscious understanding of your fiancé, his family, or of yourself.

WE'VE MET COLD FEET—AND YOU, SIR, ARE NOT COLD FEET

Sandy, Gretchen, Karen, and Carolyn all broke engagements and later married. (Sandy left her longtime boyfriend and got engaged to another man shortly thereafter. Gretchen called off her wedding, later becoming engaged to another man. She postponed that wedding but went on to marry her second fiancé. Karen and Carolyn each broke their engagements before marrying other men.)

I asked these Almost Brides (and later Actual Brides) for the difference between cold feet and frozen footsies:

I think any cold feet you're feeling should be looked into. For the most part, though, you have to go with gut instinct. If you're having a big wedding and you're nervous about being the center of attention, then obviously you're going to have cold feet, and that's not associated with marrying this person.

For me, I knew it wasn't just cold feet, because I decided that I needed my fiancé to make changes. I spoke to him about making these changes. He refused, and I knew I didn't want to live like that forever. You can't enter a marriage thinking that the person will change, so if the changes haven't happened before the wedding, and you can't live with him as he is, then obviously it's not right. [With the man I married,] there were times when I realized the magnitude of what I was about to do, and that's normal. But I don't think I ever wondered if we'[d] make it or if I [could] "put up with him" forever, and that's where it differs from how I felt with my ex. I only knew my husband a relatively short time, but I've come to realize that you don't need to know everything about someone to marry him. As long as you know his values and you have a mutual respect for one another, it doesn't matter that you don't know how much butter he likes on his sandwiches. I had been with my ex for nearly ten years, so I knew *everything* about him, and so I felt it was natural to marry him. I now see that marriage is all about learning and adapting to one another, and if that isn't happening before marriage, it sure isn't going to happen after it.

—SANDY

I have to say, postponing our wedding was the best decision I ever made. The feelings I had back in 1999 were beyond cold feet, and, although we felt at the time that we were postponing due to financial reasons, it did not feel right and I didn't feel that it was actually going to happen while I was planning it. In hindsight, I see now that had we married two years ago, we would probably be divorced now.

The timing was all wrong, and we weren't ready yet. Postponing did not mean it was over between us, and calling it off did not mean we had to call the whole relationship off; we just had to call off that step of commitment until we were ready to take it.

We are now happily married, and we both found it very easy to settle into married life. We are so much deeper, so much more stable, so much more of a couple than we were. We have been together for five years, [having] lived together almost that long. Marriage did change things, at least for me. My husband, though, doesn't feel too much has changed between us.

—GRETCHEN

With Mack, there came a distinct feeling of "everyone for himself," that there was nothing to build on or even preserve. There was history and some fondness, yes, but that could be sacrificed for our own separate goals. We were no longer on the same team.

In my . . . marriage, I'm happy to say that the opposite is true. James and I definitely feel like a team, even when we can't stand each other (for a few hours). There is a sense of partnership first—before our individual goals and existences.

Another contrast between then and now is my ability for cognitive dissonance. Then, after my engagements had broken down, I couldn't ever feel admiration and generous love for my partner, and I could only come close to being able to list his virtues when matters were calm and temporarily happy. But now, even in the worst fight, I have a strong sense of how wonderful both he and our marriage are; there's a glow in my heart (despite the temporary influx of stomach acid). Sometimes this alone can shut down a fight; sometimes it just keeps me from saying things I shouldn't. But it's always there. —KAREN

In my opinion, cold feet is different from doubts about your choice of future spouse. To me, cold feet means that you feel a bit intimidated upon recognizing the awesome responsibility that will come with committing yourself to another person for life. I feel these types of thoughts about the seriousness of marriage are normal. [Having] cold feet is not, in my opinion, having doubts about the person you have chosen to be your husband or wife. If you are concerned that you haven't chosen the right person, then you might need to reevaluate your engagement.

In my first engagement, I had frequent doubts about my fiancé. I was concerned that he wouldn't be faithful to me, that he wouldn't make our future family a priority in his life, and that he wouldn't be a good husband to me in general.

These doubting thoughts never entered my mind during my second engagement. I was, and still am, 100 percent confident that my husband is the best match for me. I never doubted his commitment to me for one minute. It was this certainty on both our parts that made all the difference in my second engagement. I am sure that I made the right choice and couldn't be happier that I found someone who will be as good a husband to me as I am a good wife to him. —CAROLYN

One year later, the only regret I have from my broken engagement is that I wavered. I wish I had stood strong and called it off instead of causing Mark so much pain. At the time, I was thinking, I'm carrying around a loaded gun and I can't fire it. Eventually, Mark fired it for me.

If you see yourself here, please fire your gun. The alternatives are much more painful—for him and for you.

A DIVORCE LAWYER GIVES SOME FREE ADVICE

Beth Monchek-Lugo, a marital and family law attorney in Florida, offers some advice:

For those who have cold feet, I would suggest that you take some time to really decide whether it's just nervousness or a sign that you should not go through with the marriage. Anyone who is getting married should already have discussed these points with her fiancé:

1. Do you have similar goals in life?
2. Do you share similar views about money?
3. Do you both agree whether or not to have children? How many children will you have?
4. Do you share the same religious views?
5. Do you share the same moral values?

In my practice, the most common issues leading up to divorce derive from these five issues.

Chapter

2

Premarital Resources

I definitely think that couples should go through premarital counseling, whether it be through a religious institution or on their own. We did (and still are), and I think it was the best thing we could do to help prepare for our marriage. I think counseling helps open your eyes to everything that's involved in marriage. In my opinion, too many people enter into engagement with stars in their eyes, thinking that everything will just work out because they have romantic feelings for one another. In reality, love and marriage can be hard work [and premarital counseling is] just more advice and information to help you prepare for your lifelong commitment. —SHARON[*]

MY STORY

A few months before our wedding, Mark and I couldn't stop fighting. One night, completely worn out by our butting heads, I plopped wearily down on the staircase of our home and suggested we talk to someone. Mark declared that counseling was an admission of weakness, or some such ridiculousness, and that "we'd work it out on our own." When in May he finally came to the same conclusion as I had—that we were in trouble—he agreed to a meeting with my therapist. But it was too little way too late. He turned to the therapist and announced that he felt "outnumbered." Then he listed the reasons he didn't think we should get married—all reasons I had given at one time or another and then pulled back on. Our die was cast.

---

*Unless otherwise noted, the women who comment on premarital counseling in this chapter and in the resource Premarital Counseling are not Almost Brides. They are either married or preparing for their weddings, and they haven't called off engagements.

FINDING HELP

But what if you haven't gotten to the point of no return? If you're wondering if getting it out in the open could help, you've got plenty of avenues to pursue. These include:

- ○ Couples counseling
- ○ Pre-Cana
- ○ Engaged Encounter/Catholic Engaged Encounter
- ○ PREPARE
- ○ FOCCUS

For more information on each of these, see "Premarital Counseling," in the Resources section.

WHY GET COUNSELING?

Diane Fields is a longtime Catholic Engaged Encounter (CEE) volunteer, along with her husband, Tom. A strong believer in the importance and holiness of marriage, she explains the importance of such a program to engaged couples by invoking the statement of a priest she knows: "He says, 'Engagement is nice, but we live on top; we don't go down underneath. We're presenting the best side. And no matter how long couples are together, something happens when you cross the threshold.' [At CEE], we challenge [people] to be who they are—to be open. Some find it too intense and leave. Some share with us later that they called it off."

When asked if she believed women with cold feet would benefit from Engaged Encounter (EE), participant Dorothy said,

If someone has cold feet, I think they should first ask themselves why they have cold feet. In my EE group we were asked to write betrothal pledges to our beloved. They said that if you did not feel ready to write one of these, your pledge should explain why this was difficult. Again, I think if you are having cold feet about getting married, you need to do some soul searching and be honest with yourself about why this is true. In this case I still think EE would be helpful, because it would put that person in a situation to spend an entire weekend focusing on [her] feelings about that relationship.

SOMETHING TO TALK ABOUT

It's important to realize that fighting isn't an indicator that your marriage will fail. More telling is *how* you argue.[1] As Michael J. McManus, cofounder and president of Marriage Savers, a group devoted to strengthening marriages and preventing divorce, puts it, marriage is "not a cafeteria where we take the dessert and go home."

Here are some of the big topics you can expect to discuss in premarital counseling.

Money

We've all heard it: couples fight about money more than they fight about anything else. According to Olivia Mellan, author of *Money Harmony: Resolving Money Conflicts in Your Life and Relationships,* it's not how much money, it's "what the money represents: dependency, control, freedom, security, pleasure, self-worth."[2]

Women who underwent premarital counseling discussed such issues as,

- How will your money be shared? Separate accounts? Joint accounts?
- What about savings accounts? Credit cards?
- Who will pay the bills?
- Will you share responsibility or will one person be the key financial person?
- How will you deal with a "mixed marriage"— between a spender and a saver—so no one feels deprived or scared of running up a debt?

Marriage

What is marriage to you? What is it to your husband? Newlywed Loretta heard a great deal in pre-Cana about the sanctity of marriage:

> What sticks out most in my mind is that your spouse is first. You should back your spouse. You should be a team. This means compromise, but you should always be there to help the other and stand by [him].
>
> This may seem trivial, but if friends, sports, and other things come first and are more important than your spouse, then you are missing the point of being married.

Sex

Married people report the most satisfying sex—physically and emotionally.[3] It's worth it to make your sex the best it can be by talking about your expectations and needs now.

Children

Two married people have to negotiate all sorts of compromises. How about when the twosome morphs into three or more? Strong marriages make for stable kids, but differences in raising (and even deciding to have) children can pull a marriage apart. Money is the only thing married couples fight about more.[4] And according to the music magazine *Blender,* the results are even more far-reaching than we thought: the reason twentieth-century American musicians are so "goddamned angry" is their parents' divorces. The music that has resulted from our society's high divorce rate ranges from Jerry Reed's 1982 hit, "She Got the Gold Mine (I Got the Shaft)" to Blink-182's "Stay Together."[5]

Family of Origin

While engaged, Loretta and her fiancé spent a great deal of time, both in and out of pre-Cana, discussing family:

> We had issues where I felt that [my husband] would put his family (brothers and mom) before our relationship and family. I have issues with his mom and it took him a long time to see why. When he finally understood and saw them, our relationship improved

tenfold. Not because I "took him away," as his mother put it, but because I finally had an ally when his mom treated me like shit.

Wedding

It may just be a day, but the planning and the headaches and the disagreement (especially when you have two vocal families and two headstrong individuals with clear ideas about their Big Day) make it much more.

Religion

Those who reported the highest marital satisfaction in PREPARE tests "saw religion as important to marriage."[6] Regardless of your level of religious involvement, the role religion will play in your home needs to be discussed.

Behavior

Giddy love will get you only so far. Are you prepared to deal with your fiancé's behavior your whole life? Is he respectful? Kind?

Communication

According to Dr. Willard F. Harley, author of *His Needs, Her Needs: Building an Affair-Proof Marriage,* "conversation in marriage does more than help us communicate and solve problems, it also meets one of our most important emotional needs—the need to talk to someone."[7]

Self-Knowledge

At the end of the day, there's you. How well do you know yourself? Are you happy with you? If you don't know yourself, how can you hope to know someone else?

Lifestyle

Courtship, fabulous as it is, is different from the day-in, day-out life of marriage. In a PREPARE study of couples, those ranked "conflicted" reported the most differences between themselves in terms of leisure activities, among other things; they also went on to report the most unhappy marriages and the most divorces.[8]

SAMPLE QUESTIONS

Here are a few of the statements presented in the FOCCUS inventory. You and your fiancé should read them separately, answering yes or no to each, and then get together to talk about the results. The point isn't to get the "right" answers; it's to be aware of issues and styles and to communicate with your partner.

1. We are in agreement about the husband and wife roles each of us expects of the other in our marriage relationship.
2. There are qualities about my future spouse that I do not respect.
3. We have discussed the ways our families solved problems and how this may affect our problem solving.

4. We disagree with each other over some teachings of the church.

5. My future spouse and I have agreed we will not have children.

6. I am concerned that in-laws may interfere in our marriage relationship.

7. My future spouse and I can talk about our sexual fears, hopes and preferences.

8. We are in agreement about how we will make financial decisions between us.

9. I sometimes feel that this may not be the right person for me to marry.

10. My future spouse and I agree that our marriage commitment means we intend to pledge love under all circumstances.[9]

WHAT IF MY FIANCÉ WON'T GO FOR COUNSELING WITH ME?

If there are issues getting in the way of a happy engagement (and you've got cold feet to prove it), premarital counseling can be a big help. If your fiancé is adamantly opposed to seeing a counselor (be it a secular therapist or a member of the clergy) even once to see what can be worked on, it should be taken as a red flag.

Refusing to see a therapist can be a sign that he isn't open to looking at himself, you, and the relationship in anything but a romantic, idealized way. It can also be an indicator of his unwillingness to do the work (and have the flexibility) to make a marriage work.

WHAT IF I'M THE ONE WHO DOESN'T WANT TO GO?

As I pointed out in Chapter One, sometimes the issue is you, and sometimes the issue is about your interaction with your fiancé. If your cold feet come from the latter, premarital counseling can be valuable. If they come from the former, as Mary points out, counseling with your partner isn't going to help.

Mary took part in PREPARE and had this to say about the program:

> I thought it was very helpful, in that it opened the door to a lot of discussion between my fiancé and me about things that we either hadn't discussed or hadn't discussed extensively. For example, when we took the

Rabbi Daniel Zemel of Reform Temple Micah in Washington, D.C., puts the engaged couples he's marrying through an informal counseling regimen of his own design. These sessions can easily be adapted for your personal (and rabbi-less) use:

First session: Rabbi Zemel asks each member of the engaged couple for the story of growing up in his or her household. "People imagine they'll live life based on life experience—embracing or rejecting it. These are assumptions the other person should hear," he says. "People tend to over-universalize the personal when in fact it's only as universal as the four corners of their parents' kitchen."

Second session: At the end of the first session, the rabbi leaves the couple with a homework assignment: each is to pick out three heroes of his or her life for a discussion at session two. They can be anyone—except parents or siblings, because they are discussed during the first session. Those chosen have included a teacher, a boss, or a writer who has touched them. The couple reveals their heroes in the second session, and one's choices—and the other's reactions to them—can be quite revealing. Zemel says, "I'm frequently shocked that people find out things about the other they didn't already know. I wonder, but I don't say out loud, *What's your relationship about if you're not sharing who you want to base your life on?*"

Depending on how the second session goes, the rabbi schedules what he calls "Session 2A"—a discussion of each person's favorite book. He acknowledges the difficulty in making the choice; many people aren't ardent readers, and others may read a book over and over but not consider it their favorite book (though Zemel would argue that it's probably their most important book anyway). "What book you choose reveals a lot about you," Zemel says, "and the book conversation keeps people talking and learning about each other."

Third session: Unlike the first two sessions, in which Zemel mostly listens, here he mostly talks—about Judaism. He describes Judaism as living life in a way that does honor to the past. "Judaism enables people to say thank you to their parents and mentors. People need to feel good about themselves, and one way to do that is to honor someone you love and cherish." He also discusses the history and theology of marriage by explaining the past and present significance of the wedding ring. In the past, "the ring was about acquisition and transfer from father to husband. I explain that's not what it is for us. I discuss the *Sheva Brachot* (Seven Blessings of Marriage), Creation, and the notion of 'it is not good for man to be alone.' Judaism knows we become more fully ourselves through another." Zemel explains that marriage is sacred, saying that it is the reflection of the covenant between God and Israel.

In your own third session, you can discuss what religion means to you and the role you wish it to play in your married home.

———————————————

test, we hadn't talked about whether we would open a joint bank account or keep separate ones. Most of the things on the test we had already discussed, but since we went through all the questions together after we took it, we discussed the things we wanted to talk about some more.

It reassured me that my fiancé and I were on the same page about what we wanted. It covered everything from childhood issues to sex to money. If there had been any red flags I think they would have shown up during PREPARE. Definitely it was better than not having it or preparing on our own.

A woman with cold feet would either be reassured by it or realize she was making a mistake and was right to have cold feet. . . . However, in my honest opinion, some people just aren't ready and their partner might be wonderful but they just have cold feet period. If that's the case, then they might be at a point where the test won't help.

I was engaged once before to a great guy. I mean *great*. But I was too young and wasn't ready, and I got cold feet and broke it off. We hadn't gone through any counseling yet. I think that I was one of those people who just wasn't ready.

By the time Mark and I got to therapy, we had already made up our minds. If you believe that you and your fiancé both want to work at your issues and that you can meet in the middle, I encourage you to try. As I told one woman who e-mailed me, distraught that she and her fiancé might not make it, despite all the time and effort spent to save their relationship: "You should have peace of mind knowing you did everything you could. If you and your fiancé make it through, more power to you; you're on your way because you didn't close your eyes to real issues. If you don't, take comfort in the fact that you gave it your all and walk away free of nagging doubts."

MORE RESOURCES

These books can help you get a better handle on what marriage is all about and whether your cold feet can be warmed up.

What No One Tells the Bride
Marg Stark
MJF Books/Hyperion, 1998

The Conscious Bride: Women Unveil Their True Feelings About Getting Hitched
Sheryl Nissinen
New Harbinger Publications, 2000

Should We Stay Together? A Scientifically Proven Method for Evaluating Your Relationship and Improving Its Chances for Long-Term Success
Jeffry H. Larson
Jossey-Bass, 2000

Before You Say I Do: A Marriage Preparation Manual for Couples
H. Norman Wright and Wes Roberts
Harvest House, 1997
(Christian in context)

Before You Say I Do: Important Questions for Couples to Ask Before Marriage
Todd Outcalt
Perigree, 1998
(Christian in context)

The Hard Questions: 100 Essential Questions to Ask Before You Say I Do
Susan Piver
JP Tarcher, 2000

Part 2

CALLING IT OFF

Chapter 3

How We Called It Off

No matter how much I tried to be nice, his ex-wife *hated* me! I could never understand it. He assured me they hated each other and told me not to worry about her because she was a witch. The couple of times we broke up briefly, they slept together. Apparently, if he wanted sex and didn't have a girlfriend, she was the easiest place to "get some." So I actually believed they were not sleeping together while we were together. (I was so naïve.)

One day, while he was still at work, I was washing clothes and happily playing homemaker. His ex-wife knocked on the door and told me that she was telling me "for my own good" that he was cheating on me. She went on to say she knew I deserved better and that he was a no-good loser, and she was *so* glad she finally got over him; she was seeing someone wonderful now. She said she knew that I loved their daughter and was attached, and she just wanted to spare me pain down the line, because she had been there and knew how it was with him. So I told her thanks for her concern, but that I didn't believe her, and she left.

So I calmly called him at work and said, "Are you cheating on me?" I was sure he would die laughing or be mad at me for even asking such a ridiculous question, but I had to ask. And his answer? A quiet "Yes."

I asked [him], "And you love me?" He said, "Yes." I said, "And we're getting married?" He said, "Yes." I replied, "No, we [aren't]. I'll be out before you get home."

And that was it. One minute, I'm happily planning the rest of my life, the next minute it's over. [It was] as unexpected and irreparable as if someone had died.
—KELLY

If you're still with us, it can only mean one thing: you're pretty sure it's not just cold feet.

It wasn't for me either.

MY STORY

Mark and I were thrilled when our bid on a house was accepted, but we started fighting almost immediately after crossing the threshold. Long talks cleared up nothing; in fact, it was as if we hadn't even scratched the surface of each other until we were alone in that house. I felt the end first. For weeks I walked around in a daze. I fought frequent migraines, thrashed to nightmares, and felt *wrong*. A year later, I put on my spring skirts and still expect them to fall to my hips. At the time, I didn't realize how much weight I was losing until I went shopping one day and found I didn't fit into *anything* in the boutique. I had fallen from a size four to a zero.

I asked him, often, why he thought it was so important that we marry. In April, I said in passing, "I don't want to get married. This is just too stressful," but we both pretended I'd never said it. In May, I told him tearfully that I wasn't 100 percent sure I wanted to marry *him,* but a few days later I took it back. Three weeks and two unproductive counseling sessions later, he left in the morning to play lacrosse with his sister. He said she and her husband would be coming home with him for dinner that evening.

I had a lazy morning. After a walk with the dog, I returned to a staticky message on our machine. All I could make out was, "Don't clean. I'll do it." (This was a sore point between us; it was his turn, but I usually couldn't stand the mess and didn't wait. Then I'd get pissy about cleaning when it wasn't my turn.) And: "I love you."

Bored and knowing he'd come home tired and with guests in tow, I started vacuuming. He walked in as I was finishing.

"Oh," he said hollowly. "You cleaned." I explained that I knew he'd be tired. I was upbeat. He walked past me. Somehow, I knew to follow.

He sat. I sat. I looked across the wide expanse of the dining room table at him. I waited for the words.

"I don't think I can do this," he said. "I just have too many doubts." I had said it myself, but hearing him finally agree opened the floodgates. I burst into tears.

I ran upstairs and started throwing clothes into a suitcase. I tore off my engagement ring and pitched it onto the bed. I overturned my jewelry box, dumping out all the jewelry he had ever given me. I barreled back down the steps with my bag and dropped it dramatically at the door. The dog tried to follow me out, but Mark called her sharply back.

It's a year later, and I can't remember the sound of his voice or what it felt like to kiss him. But I can still clearly see him sitting at the table in his red striped T-shirt, bent forward like a dead plant, sapped. I am happier than I have ever been, but the pain I caused him and the pain I felt that day stay in my mouth like the thick metallic taste of a dirty penny.

THE DAY WE CALLED IT OFF

Usually, it's been building for a while: one or both of the members of the couple feel, deeply, that the relationship is wrong. For all of us who have broken an engagement, the day we or our fiancé called it off is burned into our memory. The stories of others gave me strength, and I hope they will do the same for you.

I asked Almost Brides to describe that fateful day:

I went over to his house to "talk about things," mostly because he kept accusing me of cheating and saying I was spending too much time with my friends, which were both not true. In any case, I started to calmly tell him how I felt about all this, how these accusations were hurting me, and he just lost it, railing into me about how I was cheating on him! That is when I saw that glimpse of my future where this was the argument over and over again, for the rest of my life! I took off the ring, placed it on his dresser, and walked out.

—DANA

I got more and more freaked out and scared, finally calling my dad on a pay phone from work, crying. I was so scared he'd be mad at me. He told me that he loved me no matter what. So I went home and told Eric I wasn't ready. I can't remember if I told him that I was attracted to the guy at work; I think I did. He told me that if I wasn't ready to get married then we should break up. He moved out.

—ELLY

We had gone to Colorado for vacation, and I remember sitting at the top of a ridge I had climbed and listening to the Dixie Chicks' CD *Fly*. I was sitting there thinking about my life and wondering how I had let it get to this point, when the song "Let Him Fly" came on. I will never forget the overwhelming emotion that came over me when I heard this song. The sun was setting and painting a beautiful golden shimmer over the whole world as they sang those lines that gave me my life back: "But you must always know how long to stay, and when to go." I knew as soon as I heard that. I remember thinking, it's time to go.

In that one thought, I got away from him and I won back the two most important things I've ever given myself. I got my freedom, and I got myself. And nothing ever felt so good. I called him as soon as I got back into town and told him it was over. It was our one-year anniversary. It was painful for me to give up something I'd struggled so long for, but it was the most freeing thing I've ever done in my life, and I wouldn't take it back for anything.

—JODI

I came home early one day from work with bad cramps. He hadn't expected me and didn't hear me come in. I went upstairs, and there he was—in my missing silk panties, slip, and camisole, [with] his *Hustler* magazines. I don't think I need to describe what he was doing.

I thought I was going to puke or faint. He tried to explain that he was not gay—which I knew, and, frankly, I could have handled [that] a lot better, but that he was a cross-dresser. He said he'd always been that way, and if I loved him, he could teach me all about it. I said I['d] just gotten through law school and that was the last teaching experience I needed, thank you.

—ROXY

He was living in Europe. I had planned to go and stay there for the summer and intern. About a month before I was supposed to leave, I called at an odd time to leave a message on the machine. An American girl answered the phone and I asked who she was. She said she was his girlfriend. My response was, "Really? This is his fiancée, who's supposed to be there in three weeks." I think she was more mad at the time than I was. It mainly opened my eyes to what a complete jerk this guy was, how badly he had treated me for years, and why my friends hated him so much. I left her sobbing on the other end of the line with a promise to have him call me back. When he called, he was pissed I had told her we were engaged. I reminded him of the ring [and] my imminent arrival, and then told him to go to hell.

—WINNIE

Calling it off was actually pretty simple. I just finally reached a point where I said, "You know what? We're not going to go anywhere as long as you freak out any time the future gets mentioned. So here's what we're gonna do. We're taking marriage off the table. It's not an option. Let's just work on us." The actual breakup was messier. We actually broke up a week later, because the night my uncle died, he stayed out all night and fooled around with a friend of ours. He said he thought we were already broken up (an idea I still don't understand, since we were still having sex and sharing a bed).

—HEATHER

I went out for my birthday with a guy from work. He kissed me. I felt things when he kissed me that in five years I didn't feel with my fiancé. I realized that if I could feel this way about someone else and not about him, I needed to think about that. So I waited a few days to get my head together. Then I went to his house and told him I thought it best to post-pone things. He told me [that] if we were going to postpone it, we weren't going to get married. I said okay and handed him the ring and went home. That was it.

—SUSAN

It was May and the day after his birthday. I waited till then because I felt like I didn't want to ruin his birthday. I wanted to do it in person but it just wasn't possible. I told him I didn't want to be engaged anymore. He got hysterical and started screaming at me over the phone and cry-ing. I don't remember all he said. I do remember him saying that his mother and sister hated me. I can't remember if this was that day or a later hashing-it-out phone call. He did tell me during this phone call that he couldn't father children—that he had been told years before that he would never father children. He had never mentioned this before. Somehow he thought this would elicit sympathy. It had the opposite effect. I felt betrayed. While we dated, he managed to have a seizure and get himself kicked out of school. I was taking care of him in many ways. He spent nearly all of my saved-up college money on himself for necessities like soap and snacks for his dorm room. This was just too much.

—ABBY

[We had a big fight and] I ended up "falling" halfway down the stairs. . . . Brad eventually calmed down . . . and apologized and I ended up going back home with him. But the damage had been done. . . . Everything proceeded to deteriorate after that. . . . He didn't love me anymore. In fact, I'd keep asking him. I begged, cried, pleaded with him to just tell me. Just to say the words that he did not love me. If he'd just say them, I felt like I'd be able to walk away. But I still couldn't. He never did say the words.

Then my grandmother had a heart attack and I called to tell him, and the only thing he said was, "Well, sorry." I couldn't believe he was being so heartless. So I told him I didn't ever want to speak to him again. I went home to be with my family for Thanksgiving. When I came back, I had changed my mind. We called the wedding off officially and it was an embarrassing experience for me. I pleaded with him to keep trying—we could work things out. He said he didn't want to but we could be friends. . . . We still fought and argued, but the abuse had stopped. He walked away from everything unscathed, and here I was with nothing but depression, anxiety attacks, and insomnia. Yet I still couldn't let go. We spent the next six months continuing to go back and forth. Eventually we started sleeping together again. Brad told me that he still cared about me and wanted to try. Then, three days later, he wasn't sure again. Finally, I decided to take my niece on a cruise.

I went on the cruise and had the time of my life. It's weird. I never thought that a week could change someone so much. That week I spent away from him, away from home, away from all the pressures, was a miracle cure. I was around other people. I had been locked away in my apartment for close to nine months speaking to no one except Brad, my one really close friend where I lived, and my family. Being around other people who found me attractive and fun and laughing like I hadn't in months did something for me that no psychiatrist, friend, parent, or anyone else had been able to do. It gave me back my self-confidence. It made me realize there was a whole world out there that I was missing. It made me realize that I was not only going to be okay without Brad, but that I wanted to be without him. It was the most liberating feeling I have ever had.

When he picked my niece and me up at the airport, he tried to hug me and give me a kiss hello. I didn't want him to. At that moment, I knew I would be okay. I knew that no matter what happened, whatever this life held for me, I would be okay. The anxiety attacks stopped, I was able to sleep, and I was no longer depressed. I went back to work and transferred to a different building so I wouldn't have to see him. The ironic thing is, Brad says [that during] the week I spent away, he had made up his mind that he really wanted to try and work things out—that he wanted to be with me, and that he wanted to be a better person for me.

Just like him: too little, too late.

—CAROL

Within a couple days of wearing it, my engagement ring began to feel like it weighed ten pounds on my finger, and every time I thought about having children, I felt like I was going to pass out. I was so stressed—not about having them, just [about] having them with him. I had visions of my children being bitter because they never had any fun because their father never showed them any emotion and was always complaining about something. It just seemed like the most horrible thing in the world to me, and when I tried to envision myself with him in ten years, I thought, something's gonna break here, and I didn't really see him changing, because he didn't want to change. Therefore, it was going to be me, and I enjoyed life too much to become bitter and negative. I knew that in order to be happy with my life again, I was going to have to break it off.

It's so ironic that I left the person who [had] snapped me out of my depression and made me want more out of life, because he didn't know how to enjoy life himself. I had tried to convince him to seek therapy [with me or separately]—to no avail. I knew it was over, I just couldn't do it any longer, and that as much as I cared for him, I couldn't make him happy. He needed to be happy with himself and learn to love himself before he could love anyone else and be happy with his life.   —AMY

We had split up and gotten back together twice before we got engaged. Each time, we had waited to break things off until we had the opportunity to do it face to face (it being a long-distance relationship and all), since we [each] thought the other person deserved that much. So I wanted to end our relationship face to face. Unfortunately, that meant waiting until the day he got home from being overseas for six months. I didn't want to do it that way, but I couldn't think of any better plan. So after his family and I picked him up and brought him home, at the first moment we had alone, I asked him to come sit on the couch with me. I couldn't even bring myself to say the words; I had been dreading that moment for two weeks. I think he had a little bit of an idea what was coming; I hadn't been able to entirely hide it over the phone. He saw the look on my face and figured it out. He was the first one to actually say, "We're breaking up. For good this time." I just nodded and waited for his reaction. He wasn't as depressed or pissed off as I thought he would be (so I know this didn't completely catch him off guard). He was angry and frustrated and had a lot of questions (*Why?* being the main one, though I think he already knew). He wanted to know if I had cheated on him at all, and I said absolutely not. Finally he just went driving [and] picked up one of his sisters so they could go bitch together.   —MATTIE

My best friend, the one who had set us up, called me. She was very upset. She had just found out from someone else—I don't remember who—that he had been cheating on me. I was very upset. I thought I was going to marry him. But since I wasn't going to have sex with him until then, he had to find someone else who would. My friend was also scared for herself because my ex did have a history of violence. While I was on the phone with her, he came over. And he had his ex in the car with him! The person he was cheating on me with was with him! I told my mother not to let him in the house, but he pushed past her. I yelled at him, called him everything under the sun, and threw the ring back at him. I told him to leave me the fuck alone and to never attempt to contact me again. He then drove off in a rage. He tried to get mutual friends of ours to convince me to take him back, but I would have nothing of that. —DANIELLE

At the time, I was traveling [for] about a week every other month for work. He *hated* my traveling, as it took time away from him. Big fights would ensue, so I learned to not tell him until the last minute, so I could lessen the fighting time. The last conversation went like this: he asks me, "What are you doing this weekend?" (It was Wednesday.) Me: "Uh, I'm going to visit [my friend] Judy." Him: "What?!" I repeat myself about where I'm going. A fight ensues, of course. Then he says, "If you're never going to marry me, then just get out of my life so I can find someone else and at least be happy." At that point, the lightbulb *finally* went on and I thought, you know he's right. It is *time to leave.*

I stood up, looked him in the eye, and said in a very calm voice, "You're right. Goodbye." And I walked straight out the door, got into my car, and drove home.

And that really was it. —DEE DEE

[In the first engagement,] I had feelings for someone else I had met at a party. It was difficult [to break it off]. My family loved him—adored him, I should say. I was actually seeing both guys, which they both knew because I told this ex that I needed some space and time. He didn't give me space and was constantly up my rear. Whenever I went to see this other guy, who my parents hated, I always told them I was really with my ex. Eventually it became too much for me and I needed to end it with my ex—and I did.

[Ending the second engagement] was much more painful for me because it was out of left field; I had no idea. He came over one night and told me that he needed space. I was devastated but eventually let him leave. I questioned everyone who knew him about what was going on and no one talked—until one day his cousin's girlfriend told me that his ex was coming home to New York. I lost it. I actually got her phone number and called her mother to find out for sure and it was only confirmed. My life and my heart shattered into a thousand pieces. I immediately paged him, got him out of his house, and confronted him. I remember that I was shaking, and eventually he admitted that he was going to get her but that he wanted me to wait for him, [so he could] see if he was making the right choice! —ELIZABETH

I couldn't do it. I started wearing my engagement ring on a different finger [at] first. I had stopped making any plans. Then I just called the hall and the DJ to ask for [the] deposits back, and gave him the ring back.
—JENNIFER

I asked him to come over Saturday night because I wanted to talk to him about something. He agreed. He told me he had to work, and after work he would come over. When work let out, instead of coming over, he went straight home and went to bed. When I called his house to talk to him, his mother answered the phone like [she was] his secretary, telling me he was asleep and that he would have to call me another time. That did it! Boy, was I mad. I called him on Sunday morning; he wasn't awake yet. And so I waited until Sunday afternoon at about 3 o'clock. He still wasn't awake. I asked them to wake him and said it was an emergency. He got on the phone and he sounded really groggy. I was in tears at this point. I asked him why it was that he didn't love me the way my son's dad loved his girlfriend. I went on a total rant. I said, "Do you even care about hurting me?" He said, "No, I don't. I don't love you anymore. I want to call off the wedding." I could not believe what I was hearing. I said, "Are you calling off the wedding or the whole relationship or both?" He said, "Everything." —DIANA

After a blowup, he came to my house and [then] we went back to his house. His parents sat me down and told me that my attitude was unacceptable, that my family and I had no class, and that their son had decided that the wedding was off. As if their son could decide to wipe his ass by himself. I took off the ring and handed it to his father and said, "Here. I wasn't marrying your son, I was marrying you." Then I walked home, crying.

—NAOMI

I wasn't even thinking about the wedding when I told him he had to leave. I was just trying to make him stop hitting me. When he left, he sneered that I was never good enough for him to marry. I honestly felt we could talk about things and resolve them when he calmed down. He was being really awful, so I called his mom and told her to come and get her son, [and] then I started packing his stuff. My mom had sent my best friend (my maid of honor) over to make sure I was safe. He told me he would take our daughter away from me and I would never see her again. It was two weeks before I saw him again, and I felt awful because he had gone out three days after I kicked him out and got drunk and started a fight with a gang of guys. His face was badly injured in the fight and his family had been phoning me constantly, blaming me for it all. He used the guilt I felt to get back together with me, but I was too scared of his temper to let him come back to live with me yet.

—GRETCHEN

I asked him, while nagging him about ordering invitations, whether he didn't want to order [them] or didn't want to marry. He said, "The latter." I was quiet. Basically, it had been coming for a long time. We loved but weren't "in love" with each other, and maybe never had been; [we had] different values and temperaments. We continued (that night and the next couple of weeks) living in the same house but not speaking— not angry or sad, just in shock. I got more depressed over [my] life falling apart.

—KAREN

Basically, we would be wonderfully fine, and out of nowhere, this huge explosive fight would develop. He was going to therapy on my insistence and it obviously wasn't helping our situation, so we went together. He was totally up and down, back and forth; I couldn't handle it. He was saying that he needed to be alone to figure himself out, [and] then that we were going to be married and happy, and so on. The date for canceling the reception was bearing down and it was clear we couldn't go forward the way we were.

—LILLY

It all came down to one moment when I realized that this man was not good for me and was not my friend in any way, shape, or form. In September of 1999 (four months before I called it off), my younger sister married a man she had known for only three weeks and kept it a secret for several weeks before telling the family. Needless to say, I was devastated that she wouldn't want us to be there for her wedding and would do something so destructive. I did not meet her husband until Christmas of 1999. Sanford knew how nervous I was about meeting this guy, and he was supposed to come home with me so that I would have some comfort in this rather awkward situation. First problem: Sanford bailed on me and decided that he'd rather spend the holidays with his friends. Second problem: when I finally met my new brother-in-law, I absolutely hated him (and still do—they are on the verge of a divorce). It was so difficult. I called Sanford one of the evenings that I was home, to "cry on his shoulder" about it. His reaction was to tell me that I was a selfish brat who was lucky enough to even have a family and that I should just shut up and ignore my brother-in-law. I don't know if he lashed out because he missed having a close family or because he was a world-class asshole. It didn't really matter, because that was the final straw. He *knew* that this was tough for me, and it was at this moment that it became clear to me that he cared nothing for me and was only concerned for himself.

It was very simple. I didn't call him after [he told me I was a selfish brat on] Christmas [when I had called him for comfort]. We lived in two different cities, so I never ran the chance of running into him. He eventually called me (it was not unusual for us to not talk for a week or two, even during the best time of the relationship). When I realized it was him, I said, "Don't bother talking to me or calling me ever again. It's over." He said, "Okay," and we both hung up. That was it. —KIM

I knew that something was wrong when I didn't feel the least bit happy about what was supposed to be the happiest time of my life. I would look at others and wonder how it would feel to be happy. I had a stomachache for three weeks straight, lost weight, and had a bad case of insomnia. When the stuff about the wedding and shower came up, I knew that was it. What ultimately forced me to call it off was a quote I heard on a Canadian radio show: "Better to be alone than to want to be." I was feeling that way and knew it was over. He came over later that night and I told him that I couldn't go through with it. I was crying and very upset. It was one of the worst evenings of my life. —LAURA

It was Christmas day, in the evening, and I had decided the night before to call it off. He had gotten drunk in my mother's home to the point of vomiting and then passing out, and I decided that that was enough. We had also just spent the day at his mother's house, and I was disgusted by the whole experience. She never got dressed, [she] served us while sitting at the couch watching TV, and two of my presents were never finished; she gave them to me in pieces. I began to realize that these were the people our children would be raised around and whom I [would] eventually [have to] introduce my mother and my family to, and that I never wanted that to happen. That night, once we got back to my mother's house, I sat him down and told him how unhappy I was with the relationship and how things needed to drastically change if we were going to be able to make it together. I took off my ring and handed it to him to keep until he could get some help with his drinking problem, and told him that we would see in a bit if we could make it or not. —MARCI

About a month and a half after the official postponement (and a month before the original wedding date), his family was coming into town on a Friday. We spent the whole day arguing on the phone. He would call and tell me I couldn't come spend time with his parents (this is after we'd gone to some counseling sessions—I was trying with every ounce of energy I had to repair the relationships I had with his family). Then I would call him, crying [and] begging him to let me come over. He wouldn't give an answer. I'd call again and get mad. He'd say I couldn't come.

Finally, it dawned on me that I was disgusting myself. Why was I begging this guy to [let me] spend time with people I dreaded being around? What was wrong with me?? I called my folks and told them I was driving down for the weekend. After I threw my stuff in the car and was headed for the highway, he called and said he'd decided I could come over.

I said something to the effect of "Sorry, I got tired of waiting and now I have other plans." Of course, [to him,] that was simply a sign of how little I loved him and how I always chose my family over him. More arguing followed. (When I say argue, I mean dirty, ugly, heart-wrenching yelling— my heart still aches two years later, thinking about how hurtful the words were.) Something finally snapped inside. I had a sudden "revelation." It was like God quieted everything and said to me, "Now is the time to tell him what you've known for a long time." Please don't think I'm crazy—God doesn't usually say things to me so clearly, but I sure am thankful He did then. I told [my fiancé], "I can't marry you." His response? "Bring me the ring now." I said, "No, I'll bring it to you when I get back to town. I'm not going out of my way to do anything for you."   —TERI

We were fighting all the time, right when we moved in together. He lied to me about staying sober, and when I found his stash of empty bottles, I packed a bag and went to my mom's. The next day I pawned the ring. The worst part about it was that even though he was the one who'd done horribly wrong, he still made me feel guilty about it. We had no money, and I told him I was going to pawn the ring for groceries. No argument, nothing. I told him I wanted him to go with me. He said he couldn't, it would be too hard for him. And I wanted to scream, "And you think this is a piece of cake for me?!"

We stayed together for about another year after that, and I don't think he ever believed I wasn't going to marry him. He would always say that if my grandpa got sick we'd get married. And I just always let him believe that. But it always angered me that when I sold the ring it didn't phase him, like he knew he could get me back anyway, and nothing I said was worth anything to him. —PELLA

[He was acting strange and] I basically had to pull it out of him that he was trying to say we shouldn't be engaged and shouldn't be living together. To clarify, I asked him if he was saying that he was breaking up with me, letting him know there would be no going back from here, if that was what he was saying. He really was very unclear and wasn't able to say at that point that he didn't love me or want to marry me. He could only say that this was what he needed at that point. He also mentioned that although he was happy now, he wasn't sure that in five or ten years he would still be happy. (I think that he has a fear of divorce because of his parents' situation. They divorced when he was very young and his mother remarried a man he never was able to get along with. But I can't see never trusting yourself to make a decision because of an indefinite fear.) I have a hard time understanding how he can be unwilling to make a commitment, based on not knowing the future!

We talked a few times that week and tried to reach an understanding, but he never was able to tell me why he was doing what he was [doing], he just said it was what he needed to do. I eventually (weeks later) respected that and became glad of the fact that he did this all before we moved and actually planned the wedding or got married. —DONNA

Basically, the night he accused me of cheating on him, we were out with another couple. We had to drive all the way back home in silence (he had accused the husband of the other couple and me). We got back to his house, he got out of the car, [and] I followed, trying to get my stuff out of his house. He pushed me off his porch, threw a dead bird at me, and slammed the door in my face. The next day, I went back to his house, got my stuff, and that was the last time I saw him. There was just nothing after that night. I wouldn't go back to someone who would push/hit me. I never talked to him again.

—JOAN

Well, we were talking about postponing the wedding till we worked through some things, and finally, one night, we were talking and I said, "We can get through this, we can do anything if we love each other enough," and his response was, "No, we can't; we can't get through it, it's over." I was, of course, devastated, and it didn't really sink in right away; I couldn't cry for a long while. But finally I exploded. I started screaming at him and crying, saying we could do this, begging him not to leave me. He finally calmed me enough to sleep for a few hours, and the strange thing was that that night we slept in the same bed, and he held me all night long as we cried and talked together. The next morning I left the state where we were living and moved back to my family.

—STACEY

I finally gathered the courage to confront him regarding several issues. He denied every one of them, even though [I knew he'd been] with another woman. After he kept denying the situation, I left. In a couple days, we got together to patch things up (what the hell was I thinking?). He actually confessed to me that when he did not talk to me for a couple days, he went to a strip club. He was even gloating that some strippers were digging him.

I realized that it would not work. I took my engagement ring off, looked him squarely in the eye, and threw the ring at his head. Told him to go get fucked, and walked out. Not very ladylike, but I felt much better. The best part was when I threw the ring at his head, it hit him squarely in the forehead.

—ANDREA

ONE FOOT IN FRONT OF THE OTHER

These Almost Brides got through it, I got through it, and you'll get through it, too. One foot in front of the other, babe.

(That's your cue to turn the page.)

Chapter

4

Saying It
Out Loud

❋ ❋ ❋

One night, I met my sister in the city, as we were traveling to our parents'
house together. We stopped to get some crisps [potato chips], and the
shopkeeper said in passing, "Have a great day—life is about having fun,"
and I said to my sister, "You know what? I'm not having fun." And then I
told her everything that I had kept from my family. That night I stayed at
my parents'.   —SANDY

Before beginning the emotional work of getting over your
loss, you're going to need to unravel the complex quilt that
was your wedding. If you are early in the planning process,
you'll "only" have to deal with telling people. If you are close
to the wedding day (say, two weeks out, as I was), you'll have
the added joy of contacting vendors.

Lucky for you, the Almost Brides have been there, and
we've got some wisdom for you.

TELLING FAMILY

I dreaded telling my family that Mark and I were having serious problems. I had the irrational fear that my parents would
somehow blame me for not being good enough for Mark or
serious enough about marriage, or think I had somehow
"ruined" a perfectly good thing. One afternoon, over the
phone, the rabbi walked us through the wedding ceremony.
When he got to the part in the Jewish ceremony where the
groom pulls the handkerchief out of the rabbi's hand, sym-
bolizing that he is entering into marriage of his own free will
and signaling that the ceremony can proceed, the rabbi asked
if I wanted to have the same opportunity, as ours was to be
an egalitarian ceremony.

"Yes," I told him. Then I thought: I'm not going to be able to pull that handkerchief.

That night, I broke down and told my older brother that it didn't look like we were going to get married. Irrational fears still in place, I suggested that Mark was the only one with the doubts. David promised me that he'd help me break the news to our parents.

Still, I waited. Mark and I were in full calling-it-off talks when we went home to his parents' city for a celebratory dinner with their friends and my parents. We hung out with Mark's family the afternoon of the dinner, and I felt absolutely brakes-slamming-world-ending sick. When they got into town, my parents called from their hotel room and I stretched the phone cord taut into the living room, shut the door, and told them. Again, I neglected to mention my feelings on the issue.

"Oh everyone gets cold feet!" my mother assured me. "Even your dad!" I really don't think that's what it is, I told them. And when they saw my face at dinner that night, they knew. My father told me later that after that dinner, he and my mother were just waiting for the phone to ring with news the wedding was off.

I didn't call. Instead, a few days later, I hopped a plane home.

Weeping, I told my story to my sympathetic seatmate, (she actually said, "I know those tears," before I started in, but I didn't even need the opening). She told me how much better off I was—the first of many times I would hear that.

My parents agreed. Together, we all breathed a sigh of relief while some of us (me) cried like babies. To say my parents came through would be a huge understatement. They stayed up late, telling me just how lucky I was. When women e-mail me and say they are afraid of telling their parents and costing them all that money, I lay it on the line. Our parents only want us to be happy. Yes, Almost Brides have told me of parents being less than sympathetic, but the fact is, if your parents don't get it now, they will get it later. If they can't be happy for you, your own happiness will have to suffice. And *any* amount of money lost is worth a mistake being averted. *Any amount.* If you don't believe me, write this in large letters backwards on your forehead and stand in front of the mirror until the message gets through to you:

Any amount.

Do you know how expensive divorces are?

TELLING FRIENDS

Despite our talk of relief, my parents didn't want me to spread the word. They sort of hoped we'd figure it out in the irrational way you think your plane will maybe take off in a blinding snowstorm. I knew it was over, of course. I gave them a day, and then, in decidedly un–Miss Manners fashion, I sent a mass e-mail. I assured everyone I was fine, but I regretted having to tell them that Mark and I weren't getting married. I told them I was home with my family and I'd be in touch soon. My very closest friends called, and everyone else, respecting my privacy, sent e-mails telling me how much they loved me. As far as etiquette goes, you're supposed to send out formal cards that say,

Mr. and Mrs. Greatly Relieved
announce that the marriage of their daughter
Darling Airhead
to Mr. Fortune Hunter
will not take place.[1]

And we did that, too; it just took a few days. But I knew my friends cared only that I was okay, and the flood of replies full of love helped me immensely.

TELLING COWORKERS

I called Andrea, my supervisor, from the airport and calmly told her the wedding was off. When she exclaimed, "Oh My God! How are you?" I burst out crying. She, cool woman that she is, told me to take as much time as I needed and to come crash with her and her fiancé if I needed to. She even took my picture of Mark out of the frame on my desk and replaced it with a magazine clipping of ex-Washington, D.C., mayor (and convicted drug user) Marion Barry, to give me a laugh upon my return. Can't ask for much more support than that.

What she didn't do was tell the rest of the office. She understandably felt that this was my news to disseminate as I chose. I understandably wanted her to alert everyone and then tell them to leave me alone. (I just forgot to ask her to do so. Be sure to make *your* needs clear.) I had called one work friend, Mike, near the end of the engagement, so when I didn't show up to work two weeks before my wedding, he knew what was up. But, like my supervisor, he didn't think it was his place to "gossip" about me. This left another friend, Jim, nearly frantic, pressing Mike for details. Was I hurt? Was my family okay? Mike stood mute, a Mona Lisa of loyalty.

All this tact and diplomacy left me in the unenviable position of telling those coworkers I wasn't close to that the wedding was off—over and over. I had many conversations like this:

Reid: So how's the planning going?

Me: Well, actually, we've called it off.

Reid: (Smiling blankly.)

Me: Really.

Reid: (Smiling quizzically.)

Me: Really. It's okay. I'm okay. We just called it off.

Reid: (Smiling uncomfortably.)

Me: I'm fine. I'm cool. Do you have that document for me?

It could have been worse. It certainly was for Elizabeth:

My coworkers were the most difficult, especially with the second breakup. My family started calling me the "runaway bride," which really did hurt, but I just kind of let it roll off my back. My second fiancé had proposed on my birthday at my company Christmas party. There were about four hundred people there and all eyes were on me as he got down on one knee and proposed, and then we had a dance. For the next four weeks, people that I had never talked to before came up to me, giving me well wishes and bottles of champagne.

Then came the breakup. I was sent home from work on a mandatory leave of absence—I was too distraught to work. When I returned to work about five days later, a lot of people noticed that I didn't have my ring on anymore. It was difficult to explain to people why we weren't getting married, especially considering the circumstances. When people asked how he broke it off, I constantly broke into tears, telling them that he [had] called me from the airport on his way to California. Everyone knows how a corporate office works, especially around the water cooler: my life was up for public viewing. People always looked at me as "that poor girl" and that was the last thing I needed, like I didn't feel bad enough as it was.

HEAD BACK, CHIN UP

While you can crumble in front of family and friends, try your best to keep your cool at the office. See if you can get a few days off before you have to face the Real World again. I took off five days. My friend Debbie urged me to take more—hell, why not take my frequent flyer miles and jet off to Europe? I was planning to take a three-week honeymoon anyway, wasn't I?

But I felt strongly—and still do—that it's important to get back into the mix (and I wanted to *enjoy* the next trip I took; not walk the cobbled streets sobbing). When Debbie asked why I didn't take more time, I told her, "Even mourners only get a week, and, in this case, nobody died." (In the Jewish religion, we mourn exclusively for seven days.)

When you do have to answer the questions and respond to the pitying looks, keep a small smile on your face. I found that kept people at bay, even more than the oft-repeated exclamations of, "Hey, I'm fine." Sure it sucks that your private life is crashing headlong into your professional one. And, yes, people are going to talk for a while (till the next Big Gossip comes along). The best way to handle it is to keep 'em guessing. It's your breakup and you'll cry if you want to—just save the tears for the privacy of home.

I asked Almost Brides to describe their experiences spreading the word:

My family knew I was going to break it off, and they were very supportive. They did not want me to get married to him at all. —SAMANTHA

As far as telling people, I didn't really tell too many people we had split up. We hadn't made an "official" announcement; nor had we set a date. [When people] did ask, I told them, "It didn't work out." —AVERY

Telling my friends we broke up was relatively easy. I had e-mailed two of my closest friends and asked them if we could meet for dinner to talk—before we broke up. I wanted to discuss it with them, so they knew it was happening. I used to [send] a weekly "Wedding Planning" e-mail to many friends, so I e-mailed them the week after we broke up with the title "The Final Update" and explained that we had broken up. My parents told my extended family, who all rang me and asked me way too many questions. I didn't want to hear anyone say, "I knew it" or "I thought you'd end up divorcing." —SANDY

I told him he would have to make all the calls to the venues and our mutual friends and I . . . forced him to tell my parents. I didn't think he would go through with it. I was sitting in his kitchen when he told me [he had], and I started hyperventilating. His mother came in at that moment and said, "Don't mind me, I'm going to make a cup of tea."

That's when the anger started. I couldn't see or breathe, I was so angry at him. —ZOË

STAYING FRIENDS WITH HIS FRIENDS

Can you stay friends with his friends?

MY STORY
❖

I couldn't wing it. Truth be told, I wasn't crazy about most of them, and I didn't really miss the ones I liked and lost. The way I see it, friendship is loyalty, and my friends wouldn't have even considered staying friends with my ex, so why should his friends try to stay friends with me?

Mark had a good friend with definite designs on him. At our engagement party, she stood very close to him when she wasn't moping around, and she wouldn't speak a word to me. My friend Jill offered to take her outside and rough her up. Mark denied that his friend felt "that way" about him. Much later, we had an incredibly unproductive discussion of my own making about "last flings" and he admitted that if we had them, he'd like his to be with her. I knew I was well on my way to being over Mark when I realized two months after the breakup that they very well might be sleeping together and I didn't care. (And then I went on to date the friend I had said would be *my* last fling, if we had them. Are you keeping up?)

Mark did have one friend I really liked and admired, and as soon as we called it off, she, mensch that she is, e-mailed me, sent her condolences, and expressed her desire to stay friends. And I, klunkhead that *I* am, totally botched it.

Seeing her reminded me of him, and, as this was days and weeks after we broke up, I was still pretty raw. And I didn't hide it very well. She once said to me, "Rachel, you can't speak poorly of him with me—he's my friend, too. Just like he can't speak poorly of you to me." As I was in that world-revolves-around-me haze we all go through after a traumatic event, what I heard was, "Blah, blah, blah, he's talking smack about you."

So much for that. (Sorry, Amy.)

WELL, YOU'RE RID OF THEM

The Almost Brides surveyed all came out against staying friends with his friends. Almost Bride Samantha put a positive spin on it: "Staying friends with [your] ex's friends: No. I met these people and saw these people through him, so I never saw them again (yay!)."

Almost Bride Sandy explains the difficult dynamics:

Personally, I think it's really hard to stay friends with friends of your ex, unless you're staying friends with your ex. After my breakup, I cut all contact with my ex and therefore had to cut contact with all of his friends. His friends would e-mail me and I'd have to say, "I'm sorry, but I don't really think we can be friends, because of 'ex.'" One of my closest friends chose to remain friends with my ex, and because of his violence and so on, I had to cut her out of my life. It was a horrible experience and I felt completely let down and lonely through that. We've since become friends again, but I'll never completely trust her as I used to. It's very sad and hard for us both. We've discussed it and she now realizes how hard it was on me, but the damage has been done, unfortunately.

A few months after the breakup, I was working at an exhibition when I saw one of my ex's closest friends. He came straight over to me and started chatting. Although I had moved on with my life, it was very hard for me to not wonder what my ex was up to—and that is damaging behavior, in my opinion. I told him very little about my life, we exchanged pleasantries, and that was about it. My friends have run into my ex in the city. They've smiled at him; he nods to them and walks off. I think he's trying to behave around them and not ask questions about me.

Other Almost Brides agreed that it is hard to run into their ex's friends and be reminded of their ex.

If your ex has really solid friends and you'd sincerely like them to be your friends *also* (no poaching!) and you don't have ulterior motives (no hanging out with them so word will get back to him about how great you are doing—this isn't seventh grade), give it some serious time. Drop them an e-mail six months from now and hope for the best. And realize that you run the risk of hearing how great he's doing then.

Chapter 5

Getting Your Money Back

(and Dealing with the Ring)

❀ ❀ ❀

I didn't want to deal with any of the wedding cancellations. Thankfully, my mother was wonderful and rang them all for me. Because of my doubts, I had put off paying a lot of deposits—in fact, I had put off a lot of wedding planning. Most places gave their deposits back (we still had six months till the wedding, so they felt they had plenty of time). The videographer promised to send the deposit and didn't.

When I was booking the same church for my wedding this year, the nun said, "I remember you; you booked your date a while ago." I didn't know if she realized it was a different guy or not—I actually felt a little embarrassed, as I was getting married again so quickly. I had no doubts, and all my friends and family were supportive, but I did wonder whether the vendors remembered me, and whether they thought I was simply wedding-mad. The dress shop had my previous date on file and was confused when I went in. They said, "Maybe there's two of you"—and I didn't fix the confusion! —SANDY

So you've spread the word. It's off! Now it's time to see about recouping your material losses.

NO INSURANCE

Just as there's no guarantee you should marry, there's no insurance if you decide to call off the wedding.

Capacity Coverage Company of New Jersey attempted to offer coverage of what the insurance industry calls "change of heart," making it the only insurance firm I've ever heard of that took this kind of risk. But according to representative Carl A. Gerson, 75 percent of the claims filed came from brides or grooms who changed their minds. "Unfortunately, we no longer offer this coverage," says Gerson. "Too many change of hearts."

See? More evidence you're not alone!

As an account representative at one of the largest multiline insurers in North America anonymously explains in insurance-speak:

Wedding/Event insurance policies cannot include endorsements attributed to Change of Heart of the Insured. This is considered an uncertain risk, as opposed to those of inclement weather, serving of alcoholic beverages or poor vendor service. Although we know these events can occur, we can't predict to whom and when they will occur. The greater the uncertainty regarding the chance of loss, the greater the risk. While we can create statistical models to determine the approximate frequency of loss and claims due to inclement weather, injuries or failure to provide service, we cannot predict Change of Heart. The human mind cannot be mapped to predict intentions.

Insurance policies are a way of playing with the odds[—]safe gambling for profit, if you will. The price of a policy and its availability is based [on] the odds/chances of it being necessary. The odds that a hurricane [will hit] your wedding in October can be determined and we can assess an appropriate premium. The odds that the insured will have a Change of Heart cannot be predicted. In order to issue a policy that endorses a risk that exists completely in the mind of a human being, we would be required to assess a rather large premium to cover the uncertain odds.

Then again, who thinks of insurance back when they're forking over thousands to vendors? It's like a prenuptial agreement: Who wants to think so unromantically when it's never going to happen to you?

HOW TO DEAL WITH VENDORS

But all (your money) is not lost.

Toni De Lisa of Waldwick, New Jersey, is a master bridal consultant with the Association of Bridal Consultants, an international trade association for wedding professionals. To demonstrate the flexibility of wedding vendors, she tells the story of the couple whose wedding plans screeched to a halt when the bride was rushed to the hospital at 6:30 the morning of the wedding. Guests for the 250-guest fête were coming in from as far as Monaco. (Turns out, the bride had Lyme disease.) All but one vendor agreed to apply any monies paid to a future event, depending on their availability. All except the caterer, who had already expended money. The couple rescheduled a smaller party for three weeks later, when the bride could actually make it.

Obviously, their dilemma is different from yours. (But you could consider throwing an antiwedding party to beat all parties! At least one Almost Bride did, complete with a wedding cake topped only with a bride.)

Carol Marino, a master bridal consultant with the Association of Bridal Consultants and owner of A Perfect Wedding, Inc., in Fairfax, Virginia, explains that "vendors are not heartless; they understand and feel for the couple when a wedding is called off. However, their job is not a hobby but a sustaining business whose income they count on as well."

There's "no hard and fast rule" to getting money back, De Lisa says. But you can better your chances:

- Try for a better deal up front—though I realize this advice may be too late for you. "Check out how much your vendor is asking for and how far out he is asking for it," De Lisa counsels. "Some vendors ask for one-third payment up front, one-third halfway through, and one-third on the day of the event. Others may require a larger portion up front, or more on the day of the event." Obviously, you'll have a better chance of paying less if you haven't yet written the check.

- Be eloquent about your travail. "There are some vendors who will refund totally just because they feel so bad about the situation," says Marino.

- Work with a wedding planner. Wedding planner De Lisa believes you have a greater possibility of recouping "because the consultant brings future business to the vendor. It determines how the consultant views the next job. A couple working alone is a one-shot deal, not a recurring piece of business."

- As soon as you know the wedding is off, hit the phones. "Most vendors have nonrefundable deposits, but if they can rebook the wedding date, some will return it," Marino says. The more notice vendors have, the better their chances of filling your slot, and the better your chances of getting back your money.

MY STORY

<hr>

Going by the "more notice you give them, the better
your chances of regaining your deposits" theory,
I didn't really have much of a chance of seeing my
money again. But a funny thing happened. Our reception site, which couldn't possibly have filled our slot in
two short weeks, wrote us a check for the full amount.
It was an incredibly nice gesture and very comforting
in those difficult days.

It could be said that Oxon Hill Manor in Oxon Hill,
Maryland, knew the wedding was off before we did.
On our last visit to the site, the manager looked me
right in the face and said, "Are you okay, Rachel?
You don't look very happy."

"Tired," I mumbled, a tight smile on my face.
"Wedding stress, you know."

Then we called it off and she promptly sent a check.
In another strange turn of events, our photographer,
whom we had met but once, way back when we started
planning the wedding, called me at my office the week
after we canceled the wedding.

"I just want to tell you that this kind of thing happens all the time, and it's fine," he said. "You will find
someone else. You will."

I was a little afraid he was trying to pick me up, but,
nope, he was just incredibly sweet. He didn't offer to
give back our deposit, but his kindness was nonetheless
appreciated.

I asked Almost Brides how they dealt with vendors after they called off their weddings:

I just told all of them the story point blank and honestly without whining, and they were all very generous about working with me. The jeweler, after hearing my story, will not buy my ring back from [my ex]. I had no problem telling vendors, and actually think they are great people to talk to. They see this happen more than any of us (hopefully) ever will, so they know happy follow-up stories and certainly can tell you that you're not alone. I was very direct and honest in approaching them, though I just wouldn't want to be whiny about it; I don't think that's a good approach. Everyone has been very helpful and accommodating. I even got back my 50 percent deposit from the rehearsal site.   —CHRISTINE

Dealing with vendors: I didn't do it. My dad took over the responsibility, since he knew I wasn't going to want to explain everything. We had only booked the church/reception place and the photographer at the time, so there wasn't much lost. We didn't get any money back from the photographer, and the church refunded our money. I think we lost our deposit at the reception hall.   —SAMANTHA

My best friend, my family, and his family did all the work calling the wedding off. He kept all the money from the deposits we were able to get back.   —GRETCHEN

All of the vendors were very nice and understanding—even the ones that didn't refund my money. They were professional and all seemed experienced in handling brides who had been through these breakups. I would use any of them again.   —SOPHIE

My father was a paving contractor, and he paved the parking lot of the reception hall for the deposit.   —ELLY

ANYBODY NEED A WHITE DRESS WITH A VEIL?

You're stuck with a rather lovely, possibly flouncy dress in that unmistakable white or cream that shouts "Wedding Day!" Getting rid of it probably won't pad your wallet, but it could do your soul a lot of good.

Consider Donating Your Dress

Making Memories
www.makingmemories.org
Making Memories Breast Cancer Foundation, Inc.
P.O. Box 92042
Portland, Oregon 97292–2042
503-252-3955

Making Memories sells donated wedding dresses, bridesmaid's dresses, mother of the bride dresses, shoes, and accessories and uses the money to make the dreams of women with metastatic breast cancer come true. Your tax-deductible donation could be reincarnated as a trip to Disney World for a dying mother and her family.

The Bridal Garden
122 E. 29th Street
New York, NY 10001
212-252-0661

This discount bridal salon donates its proceeds to Sheltering Arms, one of the oldest child welfare agencies in New York.

The Glass Slipper Project
www.glassslipperproject.org
312-409-4139
info@glassslipperproject.org

The Glass Slipper Project collects new and almost-new formal dresses and accessories and provides them, free of charge, to Chicago high school students who can't afford their own. They wouldn't want a flouncy wedding dress, but they could take your bridesmaid dresses or less wedding-y wedding dresses. They are especially in need of dresses in size sixteen and over. Contact the project for information on donating.

If You Want to Sell Your Dress

While it's not generally possible to recoup the full purchase price for a wedding dress, you can cut your losses somewhat by offering it for sale.

On-Line Auctions. e-Bay (www.ebay.com) offers an easy way to get that dress out of your closet. A recent search of the site turned up over a thousand dresses for sale (granted, some of them were for Barbie dolls). Don't expect to make back what you spent, though; e-Bay is an auction site, and dresses often go for lower than $200.

Consignment Shops. Again, this route is not likely to be a huge moneymaker, but you should recoup a portion of your losses. Consignment shops give you a portion of the price of the dress—when it sells, not when you drop it off. One I checked with started by selling the dress for a quarter of what I bought it for and then took half of that. But Almost Bride Sophie is confident she'll make some money because, while the consignment shop keeps half of what the dress brings in, the proprietor is "asking almost twice what I paid for it, so I will get most of my money back."

If You Want to Be Creative

Sure it was born a dress. And butterflies are born caterpillars.

Have It Made into a Quilt. Several brides I know had their precious wedding dresses made into quilts, the better to keep the memory close. Why not make your own quilt with friends? In addition to pieces of your nonwedding dress, include scraps of fabric from solo travel, strips of your favorite falling-apart baby blanket—any bits and pieces of life that make you feel strong and taken care of. Wrap it around you when the night gets cold—or when you feel like eating cereal for dinner and watching a chick flick, unapologetically, on the couch. Independence comes in many colors.

Remake It into an Evening Gown. This is still my plan. I love my wedding dress—a very simple fitted sheath, but, unfortunately for me now, obviously a wedding frock. For the one-year anniversary of what would have been my wedding day, I cashed out my frequent flyer miles and spent a month in Vietnam. Before I left, I heard about Hoi Anh, a fishing village with two hundred tailors. My hope was to bring my wedding dress with me and let the locals make it into something a little more kicky. But it didn't work out: even though it's a sheath, it was too heavy to schlepp around for a month. Now I'm hoping to parlay my book into a free tailor visit, courtesy of *The Oprah Winfrey Show*. How about it, Oprah?

THE NITTY-GRITTY

Pull up a chair. There's a lot of doing to un-do a wedding, but the following list will help you get organized. Don't be afraid to pass off tasks; others will be glad to help you. I've noted which jobs you need to do and which can or should be done by others.

Those who were planning to host some events (like the shower) should be the ones to call and cancel.

The following is my nitty-gritty list.

Home

Bride: if you share a home, separate your bank accounts and take your name (or his) off the utilities and lease.

Contact Bridal Party

Bride: call your bridesmaids and leave the groomsmen to him.

Wedding Announcement

Bride's family: if you sent an announcement to your local paper, have a family member call to cancel it.

Vendors

If the bride: call them. Be up front but sympathetic about your predicament and ask, nicely, if you and the vendor can work anything out. Check your contract to see if it offers money back in case of cancellation by a certain date.

If the bride's family or friends: have your family or friends call them, cluck sadly, and be a bit more ballsy in trying to get back deposits.

If the groom: leave it to him and go on your merry way.

For a worksheet with a complete inventory of vendors, see the List of Vendors to Cancel following this section.

Officiant

Bride's family: ask them to call the officiant and explain the situation and thank him or her for understanding. Ask your family to let him or her know that you will be in touch when things have calmed down some.

Shower

Bride's family or friends: have family or friends cancel the restaurant reservations. They then need to call the individual guests and tell them the wedding is off. If the shower has taken place, ask them to gather the gifts and put them in a box to deal with later. There is no consensus on whether shower gifts need to be returned. This is one aspect of the unplanning that can wait till the bride has her head together and can decide how to proceed.

Invitations

Bride's family: let your family keep you far away from this painful task. According to Miss Manners:

If formal invitations have been issued, they must be formally recalled:

Mr. and Mrs. Greatly Relieved
announce that the marriage of their daughter
Darling Airhead
to Mr. Fortune Hunter
will not take place

If wedding announcements have been engraved or printed, thrifty Miss Manners suggests you make use of them by correcting them with a pen so that they read:

Mr. and Mrs. Greatly Relieved
have the honor of announcing
that the marriage of their daughter
Darling Airhead
to
Mr. Fortune Hunter
will not take place[1]

If they've been ordered but not yet picked up, cancel the order.

Honeymoon

If the bride: if it's early enough, use your honeymoon tickets for a vacation with a friend. Suck up the $50 or $100 charge to change the destination—unless you can handle the honeymoon suite at that all-inclusive resort. (If anyone asks you in the steam room where your husband is, you can always say he's golfing.)

If the bride's family or friends: if you aren't up to a trip, ask your friends or family to cancel the trip for now. Have them ask the airline and hotel how long the tickets are good for.

If the groom: if his family is paying for the honeymoon, let him take the trip. Comfort yourself by knowing that you won't be running into him for those two weeks. Back in 1997, New York City schoolteacher Nicole Conti made headlines when she was literally left at the altar by her banker fiancé. Conti proceeded down a path different from the flower-strewn aisle she had imagined, pouring her heart out to Oprah and others on the talk-show circuit, which led the *New York Daily News* to track down her ex in Tahiti, where he had taken their honeymoon alone. Maybe your ex will be similarly embarrassed. Regardless, leave it to him and go on your merry way.

Wedding Gifts

If the bride: send a quick note of thanks for the gift and an explanation of why you're sending it back.

If the bride's family or friends: ask them to send a similarly quick, veiled note along with the gift.

If the groom: leave it to him and go on your merry way.

Wedding Dress

If the bride's family or friends: send someone to pick up the dress. Stick it into the closet and deal with it when you're ready. (See the preceding section in this chapter for ideas on unloading it.) Cancel alteration appointments with the salon.

Bridesmaids' Dresses

If the bride's friends: have them collect the bridesmaids' dresses from the salon, or from the individual bridesmaids. They should check to see if the salon will buy them back. If not, you can consider selling them on e-Bay or donating them to a good cause when you're up to it. If you bought regular dresses at a department store, ask friends to return them for you.

Support

Bride's friends and family: it's the single most helpful thing they can do for you. Don't be afraid to ask for it.

Moving On

Bride: Almost Bride Sophie suggests a unique way of closing the door to the past and moving forward.

There were still reminders of the whole thing scattered throughout my house. I wanted to be free from it, so I gathered up every bridal magazine, leftover invitations, three hundred napkins with "Sophie and Michael" printed on them and took them outside and set them on fire. I just watched everything burn, and that was my turning point. I was ready to be rid of the past and start on the future.

WITH THIS RING

The big question is, do I *have* to give the ring back? The answer isn't simple. Let me put it this way: if you're having trouble sleeping, this is the part of the book to read at bedtime.

Before we go to the law, let me tell you that I agree with Almost Bride Laura. She gave hers back. As she said, "There was no way I could have kept it."

MY STORY

I dumped the ring on the bed when I left our house. Though I had no idea about the law behind my actions, and the ring was beautiful and I loved it, I never considered keeping it. (I was surprised by how many women asked if I had—and couldn't believe that I hadn't.) Mark in turn wrapped up the engagement watch I had bought for him and sent it back to me. He put it back into the original box and tied the original bow. Seeing it was quite a punch in the stomach. Now what to do with it? I considered selling it on e-Bay, but I've recently been thinking differently. Nowadays I wear it myself. Sure it's a big, man's watch, but it's stunning, and the inscription about how lucky I am means just as much now.

LIST OF VENDORS TO CANCEL

	BRIDE	FAMILY	FRIENDS	GROOM	COMPLETED
Rehearsal dinner site					
Ceremony site					
Reception site					
Postwedding brunch site					
Caterer					
Hotel*					
Ceremony musicians					
Reception musicians					
Calligrapher					
Invitations					
Florist					
Hair stylist					
Makeup artist					
Tuxedos					
Limo					
Cake					
Photographer					
Videographer					

NOTES:

_____

_____

_____

_____

*If a block of rooms for guests or a wedding night room for the couple has been reserved.

Give It Back or Run It Over

Many people don't agree with me about giving back the ring. But then again, many do. Advice columnists, like judges, have varying opinions. Dear Abby believes the ring should be returned to the giver, no matter what. Her late sister, Ann Landers, held to the fault-based rule, as in, he who ended it loses the jewelry.[2] (We'll get to the other rules shortly.) *The Washington Post*'s Carolyn Hax, guru of the thirty and under set, advises, "Just give it back. Even if you were wronged. Which would you prefer, that you have a souvenir of his failure or he have one of your grace?"[3] Miss Manners, dubbing the engagement ring a "symbol,"[4] declared that it should be returned, though she coyly admitted that it was no less a symbol if the fiancée "ran over it with her van, melted it down, or threw it off a mountain."[5] No-nonsense Prudie, of the Web site slate.com, told an inquiring reader, "You might feel more like a lady if you sent it back."[6] (Amusingly, and up there with "Well, it could have been worse, right?" another reader wrote to tell Prudie that when she called off her engagement, her fiancé took the ring and *swallowed* it: "It was a 1–1/2 carat marquise," she writes, "and as a final gesture when walking out the door, he turned to me and swallowed it. Looked like it hurt going down. . . . He turned *very* red and tears started rolling down his cheeks, . . . but I'll bet it hurt even more upon its reappearance."[7])

I asked Almost Brides, What did you do with your engagement ring?

I gave my ring back to him. I know it was for the best to just let him keep it and do with it what he wants, but I regret it because I would like to have kept it as a symbol of what our love had been in the beginning and [as] something to remember him by. Now all I have is photos but nothing that I can really hold onto. —STACEY

I gave it back to him . . . and two years later met the girl he gave it to! Ack! —AVERY

Kept mine, and four years later he still bugs me for it back! I am planning on selling it soon. —JOAN

Took it off the minute we were finished talking and never put it back on or took a second look at it. Rudely, he also wanted a diamond necklace he got me, but I told him that was a gift and there was no way. —LYNN

Had it professionally cleaned and polished, then gave it back.

—KATE

He said I could keep it. I traded it in for another that to this day symbolizes my freedom from him. It's my freedom ring. —JODI

I sold it. It took me a while to come to the decision to sell it—I think about six months. It was an extremely frustrating process, since you get approximately one quarter the replacement value. I don't recommend selling it, since it was such a problem. I actually regret it. I don't know why, but I wish I had kept it. I have absolutely no desire to still be engaged or married to him, but I really do wish I had kept the ring. It was a beautiful ring, and the fact that I'm still single makes me wonder if I'll ever get another one or another piece of jewelry that beautiful.

I couldn't imagine that any other person would want it, for that matter. I know I wouldn't want an engagement ring that was for sale because of a broken engagement; it seems cursed. I especially *never* want to see it on another girl's finger. At the time, my cousin's girlfriend approached me about buying it and I told her no because I did not want to see it on someone else! —SOPHIE

I sold it. Got very little money, too. But [I was] glad to spend it!

—KAREN

The ring was used as a weapon by the jerk; he'd tell me to give the ring back when[ever] we'd get into a fight. So I finally told him to keep the ring until he knew he'd never ask for it back. When he could do that and know in his heart [that] he wanted me to have it, then I'd wear it again. We never did get back to that point, so he kept it. Even though I helped him pay for it. He's such a jackass! But bygones [are bygones]. I'm happy now and he has to live with himself and all the crappy things he did!

—CAROL

I didn't have one. In retrospect, it figures!

—ELLY

I gave my ring back. Since I was the one who had called off the actual engagement, I felt it was the right thing to do. And I wanted *nothing* to do with him. I would not have put it past him (and his mother) to try to sue me or sic the police on me or [use] some other overdramatic tactic to get the ring back, had I decided to keep it. Plus, other than pawn the stones, I couldn't think of a single thing I would do with them!

—TERI

He had given me a Clahdah ring (Irish ring) with a stone in the center. I sent it to him in the mail. There was no reason for me to keep it and it wasn't worth pawning, in my opinion!

—SAMANTHA

Recycled the diamond and made another ring. I did pay for the original engagement ring myself though.

—JESSICA

Sold it back to my fiancé. The jeweler offered me $3,000 for it, and my fiancé wanted it, so I sold it to him for $2,000, the reason being that he owed me $12,000-plus on credit card bills that took priority. I thought that if I sold him the ring, I'd stand [more of a] chance of getting the bills paid—and I was right. He wrote me a check to cover the bills and then some, and he bought the ring. I have no idea what he intends to do with it.

—CHRISTINE

I wore it on the other hand for a while, then gave it back to him. He tried to get me to take it back after a while. *No way!* —JENNIFER

We bought my engagement ring through a local antique dealer. We had contributed to it equally, as we shared money at the time. While I initiated the breakup, I told him he wasn't entitled to the ring, as we had paid for it equally. I got three quotes and sold it to the dealer who offered the most for it—on consignment. This means that we wouldn't get the money for it till it sold. I offered my ex a contribution of money for it now—or the offer to wait until it sold. This would mean we would have to stay in contact. So I think the best thing was what happened: he took some money for it.

Nearly two years later, the ring still hasn't sold. I guess there's not much of a market for a used engagement ring. My friends at the time were concerned the ring had bad energy, as it was secondhand. I liked to believe it belonged to someone who loved it and died, but I guess not! I'm really pleased that when it finally does sell, I don't have to contact him. I think it would have been really hard if three or so years down the track I had to contact him to divide some money between us. —SANDY

The Law

Believe it or not, there are laws regarding engagement ring returns, just as there are with any other gift or piece of property, and it's important to understand the facts—even though you might not be thinking clearly until *after* you've thrown the ring at him.

In the early days of American law, according to Rebecca Tushnet, assistant professor of law at New York University School of Law, the prevailing theory of *breach of promise* carried the day. Breach of promise to marry, as defined in one court case, "seeks the recovery of those damages 'based upon confused feelings, sentimental bruises, blighted affections, wounded pride, mental anguish and social humiliation; for impairment of health, for expenditures made in anticipation of the wedding, for the deprivation of other opportunities to marry and for the loss of the pecuniary and social advantages which the marriage offered.'"[8]

In other words, women could sue when men took back their promise of marriage because, as the prevailing ideology went, it must have been the man who called it off, because a woman with a broken engagement was left as "used goods," not knowing if anyone would ever want to marry her. Over time, these so-called *heartbalm suits* began to focus on the emotions, not the economics, involved in a broken engagement.

But the shift led to a backlash from the thirties through the fifties, as legislatures and courts decided that not only was it an uncomfortable position to be in to rule on emotions, but women were taking undue advantage of the situation. Where once they were the party to be protected, women were now "gold diggers" and "deceivers,"[9] "tarnished plaintiffs" setting "snare[s]" for their "hapless swains."[10] States passed laws prohibiting women from recovering damages for broken hearts, and the courts interpreted those laws as requiring women to return engagement gifts as well. A 1957 court case made mention of

the Supreme Court of Pennsylvania, [which,] in an opinion construing a similar statute, declared: "The act was passed to avert the perpetration of fraud by adventurers and adventuresses in the realm of the heartland. To allow [the defendant] to retain the

money and property which she got from [the plaintiff]
by dangling before him the grapes of matrimony
which she never intended to let him pluck would be to
place a premium on trickery, cunning and duplicitous
dealing. It would be to make a mockery of the law
enacted by the legislature in that very field of happy
and unhappy hunting."[11]

Courts firmly believed that legal intervention wasn't
needed in the private sphere or the family, and besides, a
woman who would go to court couldn't be that pained. Why,
"the very bringing of an action to recover golden balm for
wounded affections is of itself proof that the wound has
already healed."[12] This calls to mind the old Puritan method
of determining if a woman is a witch: only witches float. So
if you're thrown into the water, you're screwed either way.

Later, the law of the ring went one of three ways, according to Tushnet:

- *She always keeps the ring (unconditional gift).* When
  the ring is considered an unconditional gift, the
  woman keeps it in the case of a broken engagement—unless it can be proven that she obtained
  the ring by fraud. ("In practical terms," writes
  Hofstra University law professor Joanna L. Grossman,
  "that means a fiancé will only get his ring back if his
  fiancée breaks off the engagement and has, for example, written her mother a letter saying, 'I don't even
  intend to marry this guy, but the ring he inherited is
  worth a million and I intend to get it.'"[13])

- *She always has to give the ring back (strict no-fault).* No matter what, the ring had to be returned when the engagement was broken. Such "bright line rule[s]," as Grossman calls them, hold firm, no matter what the consequences. So when Miss Davis called off her wedding and her angry ex-fiancé Mr. Harris choked her, she still owed him the value of the ring (she threw the ring itself into a field after she was assaulted).[14]

- *Who gets it depends on who did what to whom (modified fault).* Most courts rule that the engagement ring is a conditional gift. The million-dollar question is, What's the condition? If it is the fiancé's willingness to marry, then the fiancée would be responsible for returning the ring if she called it off but could keep it if *he* broke the engagement.

Since the 1970s, courts have softened to the realization that "failed relationships usually involved fallible people, not blameworthy deceivers,"[15] according to Tushnet. Besides, who wants to listen to, and rule on, all those cases? In no-fault rulings, the ring returns to the giver.

This is the case in Florida where the engagement ring is a conditional gift dependent on a "voyage on the sea of matrimony."[16] Beth Monchek-Lugo, a marital and family law attorney in that state, agrees with the law. "In contract law, a contract is formed when there is an offer, an acceptance and consideration (where one party makes a sacrifice to show his or her intent to enter into the contract). If you apply these principles to the law of engagement rings, it makes perfect sense."[17]

The exception to the rule is adultery. In the 2001 New York case *Marshall* v. *Cassano,* John Marshall gave Dolores Cassano an engagement ring while he was still married to another woman. Though he did divorce his wife, he broke up with Dolores. She got to keep the ring, the courts ruled; after all, how could a man have proffered an engagement ring to his beloved when he wasn't free to do so?[18]

So if no marriage takes place (regardless of the reason), the ring goes back to the person who gave it, and the parties retreat to their neutral corners. Frustratingly—and unfavorably to women, Tushnet notes that the same doesn't hold for monies spent on the wedding: "Lawsuits for recovery of expenses not directed to the defendant, but made in preparation for marriage . . . though simple to measure in monetary terms, have generally been held to be prohibited by anti-heartbalm laws."[19] When I contacted her to ask if this is going to be different any time soon, she told me, "As far as I know, there's no movement to change things."[20]

Grossman, who followed her own counsel, suggests that "if fiancés both exchange gifts upon engagement, rather than the man giving the woman a ring, then everyone will have something to keep, and something to lose, if things do not work out."[21]

If you are hell-bent on keeping the ring, you'll need to check with a lawyer in your state and steel yourself for a court battle. Tushnet notes that "in general . . . men don't sue for the return of the ring. A woman's judgement is usually the final arbiter. That being said, a woman who is sued for return of the ring is unlikely to win. If there's a risk of a lawsuit, the best thing to do is hang onto the ring—don't sell it or throw it away. As for getting a man to surrender deposit money—forget it."[22]

And if you want to *ensure* that you get to keep the ring, Tushnet told me, "the best thing to do is to marry the guy. After marriage, almost every court will consider the engagement ring and marriage ring to be the woman's separate property, and so its value goes entirely to the woman in any divorce settlement."

(This is the part where I start shaking you.)

Yes, the ring is beautiful. (I, who never wanted one at all, loved mine.) But are you nuts? Before you start what could be a long, drawn-out, and ultimately fruitless battle, ask yourself, Am I like Almost Bride Dee Dee? Be honest with yourself and think beyond your fresh, hot hurt:

I'm almost embarrassed to say I still have it. (Hanging head with shame.) Even worse, it was a set. The wedding band wraps around the engagement ring. Together, it really is gorgeous. He wanted it back. I refused to give it to him. I told him it was a gift, as he had given it to me on Valentine's Day. I was definitely being vindictive, even though I was the one who called it off. I knew all he wanted to do with it was sell it. For some strange reason, I felt that if he sold it, it really was "over." As long as I had the rings, well, maybe there was some chance somewhere that it might work out. Total emotion talking, certainly not my head, as I would *never* have gotten back with him. Periodically, I would wear it as a dinner ring on my right hand.

Once I started seeing my now-husband, that stopped. So I still have it in the safe deposit box; I can't wear it now that I'm married. I have no idea what to do with it. If I sell it, whatever money I get would seem like it's from him, and I'd feel weird about buying anything with it.

Chapter 6

Why Marry in
the First Place?

[I wanted to marry him] for the same reasons I wanted to date him: he seemed so funny and especially cute. He made me laugh and I felt good when I was with him (we worked together). We had a lot of fun together, even at work. When we hung out outside of work, we just clicked. He just seemed so sensitive and caring. He was really sincere. And also the way he was with his family. He was one of five kids (the youngest) and his family was soooo important to him. I hadn't met any-one like that. Most of the guys I had dated seriously before him had divorced parents, siblings they had never seen. I am very close to my family, and it felt good to be with someone with the same values. Also, his family welcomed me into their home right away. I also think, look-ing back at it now, I was in love with being in love. I was so caught up in it, it was very powerful to me. —SAMANTHA

A helpful first step for processing our torrent of emotions is understanding how we came to be Almost Brides. Why do women marry, anyway?

MY STORY

One summer day at a café in the center of Amsterdam, Mark and I talked, again, about getting married. I had met him in Europe with big news: I was ready to get engaged. After the fact, it looks like yet another flashing red light I zoomed through, but back then, I didn't want to marry him. He likened the process to going through a tunnel to come out the other side—to where we, happily, already were. I asked him then, and many times before and after: Why go through the tunnel if we're right where we want to be?

Maybe I'm unusual, strange, a freak. I've never stressed about being unmarried. Unlike my other single girlfriends, I never waited impatiently for the appearance of "The One," and my best friend from childhood recalls my unbidden declaration at age eleven that I'd never marry. But I fell in love with Mark, and marriage was important to him. I figured I was strange not to want to marry him (since I did want to spend my life with him), so I went along. But I found myself asking him, constantly: Why?

Why did we have to fight with our families and each other about the number of guests who would be allowed to watch us take our vows? Why did we have to spend a boggling amount of money on the "right" flowers and five hors d'oeuvres when all we wanted was to grow old together? Why did we have to make it "official" when we knew in our hearts that it was already?

One night, before our hell broke loose, we watched the movie *Chutney Popcorn* on video, wrapped up in each other on the couch. In the film, a woman can't have children, and she and her husband desperately want them, so her sister volunteers to have their baby. It's hardly an easy decision; the volunteering sister is a lesbian whose lover is against the enterprise, for one. Mark piped up that he'd like to pass on his genes, even if I couldn't help out. That pretty much blew my mind, which led to yet another discussion about getting hitched, and, holding me tight, Mark said, "I don't think you're ready for marriage."

"What does that mean?" I asked, pulling away to look at him.

"You're not ready to merge," he said gently.

"Hell, no," I retorted. I didn't want to merge. We were individuals who were forming a life together to support each other and love each other and inspire and enjoy each other, but, no, I didn't want to *merge* with him.

As with all these discussions we had as the wedding drew closer, I feel now that this was the one that signaled the beginning of the end. I couldn't believe the thoughts he expressed—we weren't forming our own family; rather, I was joining his. That kind of thing. To this day, I imagine he shakes his head when he thinks of me. "Poor thing," he probably thinks. "So independent, so *feminist*." And, as I think of him, "so wrong."

So much of my relationship with Mark leaves me still shaking my head in disbelief a year later. But the strangest part of the whole experience is this: breaking up with Mark—two weeks before a wedding I never wanted—has changed my mind.

It's as if my life is divided into Before Mark (BM) and After Mark (AM). BM, I was that eleven-year-old, trumpeting my need for independence and my disdain at involving God and state in my affairs. AM, I look around at the good, solid marriages and feel a tightening in my chest. Me, too, I think. Me, too.

BM, what led me to declare to my friend that I'd *never* marry? It wasn't my home life; my parents have

been happily married for thirty-seven years. It wasn't a
lack of interest in boys or men; I've always had that.
And what happened AM? I went through the most
traumatic experience of my admittedly sheltered life.
For a good several months, marriage was an idea I didn't
want to think about at all. Then, as the pain faded, it
was as if the scales fell from my eyes.

WHY MARRY?

What is it about marriage? Why *do* we involve God and the
state in our most intimate affairs? In trying to answer this
question, I made the local Washington, D.C., library my
home. Every week, I carried a stack of feminist works home.
Every week, I anticipated a librarian stopping me as I wob-
bled under the weight of my books to tell me that there was
a limit to the number I could check out. But they never did.
(Thank you, Cleveland Park library.)

I read on the couch, in the tub, on the train. When I wasn't
reading, I was thinking about my choices and watching others'. I knew and learned more about the roots of marriage,
the family ties, and the goat dowries. I was hungry to know:
How did we get from yesterday's economic and sexual neces-
sity to marry to today's internal *need* to pledge ourselves to
one man for the rest of our lives? Why is Almost Married Jill
not alone in seeing marriage as "a routine that has been
engraved into our society as the norm"? In my reading and
my musings, nine basic reasons kept coming up. They are:

1. *Money.* In the 1920s, Virginia Woolf inherited a good lump of money from an aunt. The inheritance gave Woolf a freedom known to few women at the time. Because of it, she wrote, "I need not hate any man; he cannot hurt me. I need not flatter any man; he has nothing to give me."[1]

While Woolf wanted nothing more than to write, most women in the twenties and beyond assumed that the men in their lives would feather their nests. In 1952, Simone de Beauvoir complained that this thinking only hurt women:

> Parents still raise their daughters with a view to marriage rather than to furthering her personal development; she sees so many advantages in it that she herself wishes for it; the result is that she is often less specially trained, less solidly grounded than her brothers, she is less deeply involved in her profession. In this way, she dooms herself to remain in its lower levels, to be inferior; and the vicious circle is formed: this professional inferiority reinforces her desire to find a husband.[2]

A decade later, Gloria Steinem documented the same phenomenon. When she famously took a turn as a Playboy Bunny in the Playboy Club in New York in 1963—what the Playboy manual called "the top job in the country for a young girl," a fellow exhausted Bunny confided, "After three months of this, I want to get married. Guys I wouldn't look at before, now I think they aren't so bad."[3]

Which brings us to the present. In 1985, Susan Faludi pointed out that the more money women make, the less likely they are to rush to the altar.[4]

2. *Societal acceptance.* Marilyn Yalom, author of *A History of the Wife*, explains:

> Once upon a time, women wore the title "wife" like a badge of honor. To be a parson's wife, a baker's wife, a doctor's wife told the world loudly and clearly that one had fulfilled one's "natural" destiny. It spoke for legitimacy and protection in a world that was proverbially unkind to spinsters. Whether one was happily married or not, the wedding ring, in and of itself, was a measure of female worth.[5]

The term *spinster* originally meant nothing more than one who spins thread (not an enthusiast of the aerobic cycling class), and antimarriage writer Jaclyn Geller urges unmarried women to reclaim the word.[6] But Germaine Greer explains why no one really wants to:

> There was always a sickly cast of rejectedness about spinsterhood, which was seen not so much as a woman's own choice as the result of not having been chosen. The stereotype of the spinster was that she was a starchy, forbidding creature that men could not warm to. The less she had of male attention the more angular and repellent she became. She began life as a wallflower, the girl nobody danced with, and she continued as unbought merchandise "on the shelf."[7]

No one wants to be considered "angular and repellent," which leads us to point number 3.

3. *Proving one's attractiveness.* If you stacked all the magazines and books that tout methods for "getting your man" end-to-end, they would easily reach any pie in the sky. Reviled as it is, Ellen Fein and Sherry Schneider's *The Rules: Time-Tested Secrets for Capturing the Heart of Mr. Right* reached the top of the *New York Times* bestseller list shortly after it was published in 1995.[8]

Inherent in one's attractiveness is sexuality. And according to Peggy Orenstein, author of *Flux: Women on Sex, Work, Love, Kids and Life in a Half-Changed World*, the next link in the chain is no less than one's sense of self:

> After four years of talking to women, . . . a few things have become clear. The first is fundamental: There's a critical connection between sexual agency and a lifelong sense of self. As [one young woman she interviewed] herself attested, it's imperative that girls feel a strong sense of sexual self-determination from the outset, that they understand that sex is not about pleasing boys or competing with friends but ought to grow from authentic desire, feelings of intimacy, mutual respect, as well as from an innate right to pleasure. "It's absolutely key to esteem issues for me," she had insisted when we first met. "If you're comfortable with your body, you're comfortable with yourself. If you feel like you deserve all this pleasure in bed, you start to feel like you deserve it other places too."[9]

Today, according to Orenstein, women in bad marriages "preserve the peace at the expense of their own well-being until it becomes intolerable." They then ask for divorce—in greater numbers than men do—to regain "their sense of self" and "even those that were abandoned by their husbands described a sense of renewal."[10]

So if marriage can be so bad that you can lose yourself, why do women rush in?

4. *A way to avoid growing up.* One interesting theory, floated by Betty Friedan, is that marriage keeps women from growing into adulthood, and eternal childhood is comfortable. She considers young marriage "a kind of defense against intellectual development."[11]

5. *Children.* There are two ways to look at children and marriage: the prevailing ideology is that one can't exist without the other. As recently as 1992, Murphy Brown was the butt of Vice President Dan Quayle's ire for (fictionally) bearing a (fictional) child on her (fictional) TV show.

But in some circles, women have been pushing against convention for as long as they've been marching for equal rights. Emma Goldman, one of the earliest proponents of feminism and birth control,[12] spoke against marriage, saying that it made of women "parasites," and declared that "if the world is ever to give birth to true companionship and openness, not marriage, but love will be the parent."[13]

It is indeed very possible that the best way to bring up a child is in a committed, loving relationship. But does that relationship have to be a marriage? A seventy-year-old friend of mine told me that she married the man she loved because she wanted children. With that stricture dissolved, she wondered aloud, would marriage die out?

6. *Unnamed fear.* Today, most women make their own money, lose their virginity before marriage, and feel pretty

damned attractive. We're all grown up, but many of us, even if we don't want to admit it, are scared we'll never marry. Some of you will remember the frightening study in 1986 that concluded that because of America's man shortage, women over thirty-five had a better chance of being taken hostage by terrorists (or was it killed by lightning or mauled by their house cats?) than marrying.

In her seminal work, *Backlash,* Susan Faludi deconstructs that myth. More amazing than proving that the man shortage was bullshit, she shows how the media basically took the false information and shot it into women's hearts.[14] The shrapnel is still there. My late single aunt used to have a message on her answering machine congratulating all callers for having won the "matrimonial sweepstakes." Orenstein describes the confident women with this unnamed fear trembling inside them as being "between pluckiness and panic at nearing 30 alone."[15]

7. *Companionship.* In *The Good Marriage: How and Why Love Lasts,* Judith Wallerstein and Sandra Blakeslee put it lyrically: "A good marriage can offset the loneliness of life in crowded cities and provide a refuge from the hammering pressures of the competitive workplace. . . . Marriage provides an oasis where sex, humor, and play can flourish."[16]

In a spouse, we're looking for a soul mate, a partner, someone to watch out for us. Geller argues that there's no reason to bring the government and the Macy's registry into such a private decision,[17] but my personal jury's still out on this. When I look at the strong marriages around me, I see something beautiful. More than the above reasons for marrying, this one resonates with me, and probably with you.

Hand in hand with companionship walks commitment.

8. *Commitment.* Why else would journalism professor Wendy Swallow, whose memoir, *Breaking Apart,* explored her painful divorce, choose to remarry, when doing so meant moving out of her home, changing her sons' schools, and blending families?[18] In an excerpt published in *Washingtonian* magazine, she writes that she'd consider just living together if she and her partner didn't have children:

> Why not just go for the romance? Tempting, but kids change the equation. If you are bringing children with you into the partnership, there needs to be an underlying foundation, a commitment. My gut feeling is that it needs to be hard to get out. Like building a vessel that can withstand a storm, my instinct is to plan for flexibility but lash it all up pretty tight.[19]

9. *Just because.* That's the one my father told me. "People marry," he told me, when I was small. "And people have kids." There wasn't really a *why.* In *Rules of Engagement: Four Couples and the American Marriage Today,* journalist Lis Harris eavesdrops on the marriages of four couples over several years, taking notes on their hand-holding and yelling, their quiet contentment and affairs. But *why?* I thought as I read their stories. Sarah and Eaton, a New York upper-middle-class couple, are one example:

> [N]either Sarah nor Eaton considered the possibility of their living with each other for a prolonged period

(as the next generation did) to see how well they would get along; an arrangement of that sort would have caused seismic tremors in the families of both of them. Instead, Sarah found her resistance to the idea of marriage lessening, and Eaton found his already primed predisposition to marry quickening. Once the idea took hold, they both proceeded toward the event with a remarkable degree of rationality.[20]

They were engaged in two months. Just because, I guess.

God and Taxes

Pamela Paul, the author of *I Do . . . For Now: Starter Marriages and the Future of Matrimony,* points out that "marriage is not a transformative act. It does not make you more successful or more balanced."[21] So why do we choose "signing on the dotted line," as opposed to just living with the one we love?

When I posed this question on theknot.com, the two answers I got were religion and the government. When we declare our commitment, we seek to make our relationships holy in the eyes of our respective gods and earn the benefits the government doles out for having done so. These include making medical decisions and benefiting from estate laws. We have only to look at the fiancées left behind when the World Trade Center was destroyed to see how the government feels about those who haven't yet married. One young man lost, James O'Grady, thirty-two, hadn't yet changed his will; he had bequeathed everything to his pregnant sister. His mother and his fiancée, Rachel Uchitel, twenty-six, "clashed" over this. Mrs. O'Grady, *The New York Times* reported, "acknowledged that 'the bottom line is, he loved her more than anyone else at the end there.' But to her family [the O'Gradys], she said knowing someone for two years is not the same as knowing them for 32."[22] So Mrs. O'Grady holds the cards; if Rachel and James had been married at the time of his death, the power would have been shifted.

Fears and Friendship

When we look to marry, we're most probably thinking about companionship and commitment. But it's worthwhile to acknowledge that the other reasons for marrying shouldn't be discounted. Bits of them still cling to us. We do think of how having someone else's money in addition to ours can make our life easier. We do wish for society's acceptance. We do like the idea of being so irresistible that a man wants to make us his "own." Some of us, the younger ones, may still be looking to avoid adulthood. We sure as hell have fears of being alone. As Orenstein writes:

> For [some] women, initially so self-assured, the vision of single life began to metamorphose around the age of thirty from choice to threat, from liberation to desperation, from a symbol of defiance to one of deviance. Some have gone so far as to call it the eleventh commandment: "Thou shalt not be single, over thirty, and happy."[23]

Perhaps our generation and those that follow us will make different decisions. Perhaps what we've gone through will change the course of our future.

We can appreciate the humor of Ellen Willis's satire "The Last Unmarried Person in America":

> Minutes later we were on our way to an exclusive interview with Ruby Tuesday, the last unmarried person in America. We caught up with Ruby, who makes her home in an empty car of the Lexington Avenue IRT, at the Union Square Station. She was a striking-looking woman. It wasn't the green hair so much as the fact that instead of the one scarlet S [for "single"] required by law . . . she wore a see-through satin jumpsuit made entirely of scarlet S's sewn together. . . . We asked Ruby why she had such strong objections to marriage.
>
> "It's taken me 15 years to get this car just the way I like it," she said. "Why should I share it with some asshole?"[24]

But we still can shake our heads at the venom in the pen of writer Lionel Tiger:

> It is . . . astonishing that . . . marriage is still legally allowed. If nearly half of anything else ended so disastrously, the government would surely ban it immediately. If half the tacos served in restaurants

caused dysentery, if half the people learning karate broke their palms, if only 6 percent of people who went on roller coasters damaged their middle ears, the public would be clamoring for action.[25]

When writers like Jaclyn Geller, author of *Here Comes the Bride: Women, Weddings and the Marriage Mystique,* and Marilyn Yalom, author of *History of the Wife,* discuss, in painful detail, the mawkish history of marriage, you and I are level-headed enough to know that this isn't the marriage we're walking away from. Yes, marriage has as its history the authority over a woman's destiny and chastity, a Church-controlled protection of procreation, business-like backroom dealings of economics and heirs. But I'm not here to smash to bits a tradition with such Woody Allenesque moments as the Romans preparing "a special wheat or barley cake . . . which was broken over the bride's head."[26]

We all have parents, grandparents, or friends with wonderful marriages. We may choose not to marry, but it won't be a choice we make out of bitterness or fear. Rather, we're here to figure out how we came close to accepting forever with the wrong man. I believe if we do that, we can go on to a brighter future, and what that future holds is up to us.

I want to use what I've learned in calling off my wedding to make better, stronger choices—choices I may not have even been aware of before.

It's the strongest legacy we've got from calling it off, and it's a fabulous one.

WHY DID YOU WANT TO MARRY?

With the nine traditional reasons for marrying in mind, it's interesting to see where some women went wrong.

I asked Almost Brides why they had wanted to marry their fiancés. Only two thought of themselves as a couple with a real future. "We were incredibly close and had the same goals in life," Lilly says.

"He treated me very well and he was, perhaps, the first man I ever dated who did," says Dana. "He catered to my every desire, he believed in all my dreams, and he wanted the same things I did."

Some others wanted to get married because of the love they felt:

I thought that giddy feeling I had around him was love. I also thought that all the things I liked about him meant he would be a good husband.

—ABBY

I was in love with him, body, mind, and soul. I had no doubts that we were meant to be together, that our love was magic and cosmic.

—TAMARA

I had never been more open and honest with anyone than I was with him. We got along very well, and I felt very loved by him. —HILARY

I loved him and his kids. —KELLY

He was fun, sexy, interesting. We had a great time together, and we did things I've never done before (picnics, long car cruises to scenic places, and such). —AVERY

I thought he was this person waiting to happen, that if I could just get him to see all of his potential, then he could be a really wonderful guy, and it was this wonderful guy that I was wanting to marry. —MARCI

Two reasons: I loved him more than anything because he made me feel loved and so special at first. And I didn't want my child to have split parents like I did. —GRETCHEN

Because he made my heart skip a beat every time I saw him. When he would hold me in his arms, there was nothing else that mattered in the world. I loved him with all my heart and wanted to be with him forever.

—STACEY

[With the second man I was engaged to], I thought he was "the one." I really felt like he was the one I had been waiting for. I was totally in love with him. —ELIZABETH

A surprising number of Almost Brides offer patently unromantic reasons for wanting to marry:

[With the first man I was engaged to], it seemed like the next step. We were together for a while and it seemed like the right thing to do.

—ELIZABETH

It felt like the thing to do. We never spent any time apart, with other people. The more time we spent together, the more it felt like we should always be like that. —ANSEL

I don't know why I wanted to marry him. Perhaps because we had been together for so long (over seven years). I supposed I didn't think I would find anything much better and I had already invested so much time. (My God, that sounds horrible!) —CAROLYN

It sounds silly, but none of my friends or family took my relationship with him seriously. I thought that by my getting engaged, people would realize how important we were to one another. I never got invitations that included him, so I thought that would change after we got engaged. I also thought I was comfortable enough to live with him forever and that no one else would be interested in me. He wasn't at all close to my family, so I also believed that he would feel like part of the family if we got married. In short, I thought I could change him, which was obviously the big no-no! —SANDY

We'd been together on and off for almost seven years. I think I just wanted to make it permanent, regardless of whether that was a good idea.

—WINNIE

I wanted to marry him because we had a daughter together [and I have a son] and I didn't want to have children with different fathers. I loved him and I knew that our relationship wasn't perfect. But I thought that by getting married we could pool our love together and make it work. I was also looking for some relief. Taking care of my children was hard work, especially as a single parent. I thought that if we got married, he would be a great help, and I wanted to share the responsibility of raising them. Additionally, his family never made my son feel like he wasn't part of the family. —DIANA

I thought it was what I wanted at the time. —DONNA

I thought we had similar goals and we were thinking on the same page.

—ANDREA

Because we were a match on paper. He would have been a good provider and a good father. The real reason was that I thought that if I didn't marry him then I would never have children. —LAURA

I thought he was the best I could do. He was very intelligent, and that was important to me. I thought he loved me, even though he never once said it in our three-year relationship. —KIM

Honestly, I felt I was getting older, too old to start over, [and I] wanted kids. —JENNIFER

Because I never believed I would do any better. I knew then completely that I was settling for the best I thought I could do. —PELLA

I think at that point in my life I would have married King Kong, had he proposed. I just wanted to be like everyone else—with a husband and a family. —NAOMI

Seemed like the next logical step to take and the right thing to do. And I was twenty-nine years old, and that neon expiration date of thirty was flashing brightly on my forehead—[as] my mother consistently reminded me. —AMY

At the time, I was ready for a *wedding,* not a marriage. Most of my friends were married. I was twenty-four and thinking it was time. He was convenient. —DEE DEE

Because he asked me. —DANIELLE

I'm not sure I ever really did, but he asked, so I didn't want to turn him down. When I said yes, I guess I didn't think of it as a serious proposal at first. —JOAN

I'm embarrassed to say. Probably because he convinced me that it was such a great idea! —TERI

STOP! IN THE NAME OF LOVE

Every time my fiancé and I fought, I sought to make it right, or I rationalized that he couldn't *possibly* hold the opinions he stated. Even as I attempted to tamp down my growing unease, I *knew* we were in trouble.

IGNORING THE SIGNS

I asked Almost Brides: Were there signs that this relationship was wrong? Did you ignore them?

I ignored the fact that I had to lose all my friends to keep him. I ignored it when he would go out to bars and I had to stay home. I ignored the cheating, lying, drinking, and the drugs. I ignored my friends' and my mom's opinions about him.

—ANSEL

Yes, there were signs. After a while, his jealousy got so bad that we were having the same arguments time and time again. It got to be so tiring. And one day, just to see what would happen, I intentionally picked a fight and I was obviously in the wrong, but he deigned to my wishes. I knew then that he was not the person for me.

—DANA

Actually, the earliest sign came when he told his mother that we were engaged. We had agreed to not tell our parents yet but he did and didn't tell me for a while. He didn't really consider what I said or thought to be important. He had a very conservative view of our relationship and thought that being the man meant he could tell me what to do and who to do it with. It didn't come out in so many words until many months into the relationship.

—ABBY

I always said I would never date a guy who didn't have a five-year plan. He had no goals or plans for the future. He still lived with his mom. When a guy is over twenty-five and still lives with his mom, chances are he'll never move out.
—DIANA

My nice underwear began to disappear, he wanted me to wear dresses and skirts more often, and I found a stash of pornography when I vacuumed one day.
—ROXY

We postponed the wedding twice. The first time didn't send up a flag because it was coming up pretty quickly and I was (eventually) okay with the postponement. The second time, when he wanted to postpone indefinitely because he wasn't sure he'd ever be ready to get married, I was just so desperate not to have wasted my time that I chose not to worry.
—HEATHER

Yes, there were a million signs! He cheated me out of rent money, wouldn't pay for groceries, [and] claimed to hate his most recent ex-wife—but they talked on the phone every day. Girls would call our apartment but say they had the wrong number when I answered, [and] he admitted [to] cheating on both of his ex-wives but somehow convinced me it was their fault. Um, yeah.
—KELLY

Absolutely. I was never in love. I was trying to make it work because he was a good guy and I didn't think I would have another chance.
—LAURA

Yes. He had a wife he was legally separated from. . . . That should've been a *big* clue, but I ignored it!
—AVERY

Signs within myself . . . that I may have wanted to stay more for security and that he loved me so much. But I ignored how I truly felt.
—JILL

So many. First of all, he and his sister enjoyed saying things like, "I was raised to be the center of attention and I'm not going to apologize for it." They said things like that in mixed company and thought it was so endearing (keep in mind he was twenty-five and she was thirty-one), but it actually summed up how he lived his life (and how his parents encouraged him to live!). He encouraged me to lie to his parents. He encouraged me to start fights with them because, no matter what I wanted, if he wanted X and they wanted Y, I should side with him. He created arguments when none truly existed. He actually raised his voice at my mother and sent a nasty e-mail to my grandfather. (I was not witness to the voice raising. He, of course, denied it and then berated me when I gave the slightest indication that I might believe my mother.) —TERI

The guy didn't *want* to be in a relationship; that was so obvious, and looking back, I can't believe that I missed it! I was a convenience for him. He made plans without me all of the time and generally didn't want me around unless I was available for sex. I saw his aloofness as his way of being independent—like it was part of his artsy personality. I also know for a fact that he cheated on me at least once. How do I know? He told me—and I forgave him. Stupid, stupid, stupid. —KIM

Yes, I ignored the fact that his drinking bothered me as much as it did, and I didn't allow myself to feel unhappy with the relationship at all, although I really was for quite some time. —MARCI

Oh, yeah. [With the first man,] I started letting myself go, not taking as much of an interest in my appearance as I usually did. [With the second,] his temper, phone calls [when] he wouldn't tell me who it was, and, oh God, the lies!!! —ELIZABETH

Yes. The fights when my feelings were *never* considered were probably the biggie. And when the behavior just got out of control, I chose to justify it then.

He was just not behaving normally, but I didn't see it then. There was mild physical abuse that there was always an excuse for. —PELLA

I saw the signs of his temper and his lack of respect for me as well as the signs that his family would always have his loyalty before our daughter and me. —GRETCHEN

I didn't adore him, sex wasn't good, I was depressed; neither of us felt like planning a wedding. —KAREN

I never really ignored the signs; I just always thought that we could work it out. I think I downplayed these issues ("swept them under the rug," as my mom would say), since we were together for so little time during the year. I didn't want to worry about issues during our scarce time together. But eventually I realized that many of our issues were "deal breakers" for our relationship and that all of them together would be very difficult to manage for a lifetime. —MATTIE

The fact that his parents controlled him so tightly he was terrified of them, and if they said "jump," he jumped. I hated this and told him so, but he sided with them at every turn in the road. —NAOMI

Yeah, I should have paid more attention to the fact that he always wanted to be in the spotlight—never me. —ROBIN

Of course, but I was turning thirty and that expiration date stamped on my forehead was flashing so brightly that it blinded me from all the signs. [I didn't consider] his refusal to go into counseling for his attitude [or] my refusal to look into the future farther than the ring on my finger. [And there was also] my foolishness in not examining our relationship objectively and listening to others' advice. —AMY

Yes, he was not as happy as I was. I ignored it and thought that it was just him. —STACEY

Absolutely. [There was] the fact that he was not a responsible individual. I don't think he respected me, or he wouldn't have started the verbal abuse. He did not support me in my life, going so far as to fight with me every time I had to travel for work. Well, one of us had to work! Also, he would lie to me about his having a job. Twice I discovered that he didn't have a job at all. He was very jealous about my time away from him. All in all, not a healthy relationship.   —DEE DEE

Early on, if I upset him he would go to ridiculous lengths to show me—like bashing walls or trees until he bled. I ignored that because I thought that if he wasn't hurting me, it didn't matter. Hindsight: what a wonderful thing!

—SANDY

Yes, [I had] a bad feeling about the whole thing. He didn't respect my feelings on very important things—like fondling me in public.

—DANIELLE

I saw signs. I just chose to ignore them because I didn't want to confront him.   —ANDREA

DO NOT PASS GO, DO NOT COLLECT A DIAMOND RING

Why do we ignore the signs of a bad relationship? If someone ran over your foot as you stepped off the curb (and especially if he took the trouble of backing up so he could run over it again and again), you'd sure as hell speak up. If a colleague or a boss maltreated you to the point of tears or severe rationalization, you'd yell, or tattle—or look for another job.

Author Dalma Heyn writes of the tendency of women to "submerge a vital part of themselves when they marry."[27] I believe that we don't even wait till we're "altered at the altar."[28] In many cases, it doesn't even take till we've got the diamond on our finger. Rather, it's the hope of becoming a wife. Heyn speaks of the Witness, a ghostly specter originating in conduct books that emerged in the late seventeenth century and whose ghastly grip is still so hard to shake. The Witness is who we're referring to when we say "they say" or "society says." Through the Witness:

> We become adept at seeing things as they "should" be through others' eyes. Through others' eyes, marriage confers upon a woman not only intimacy, identity, safety, and happiness but an inner goodness, an acceptability, she didn't have before. Through others' eyes, marriage is the culmination of a woman's quest, the proof she did it right, earned a sanctioned love, became the heroine of the story. Through others' eyes, marriage confers on her idealized qualities she didn't have before but could only dream of: "To love and be loved is to become a hero," British sociologist Annette Lawson reminds us. Through others' eyes, the vision of herself in this mythic condition of contentment is as resistant to questioning as the notion of happily ever after. A woman may "know" it is romanticized and unrealistic, she may "know" she herself views things differently, but even the children of divorce, even the oft-married and the most cynical about relationships cling to the myth of happiness of the married state and anticipate a happily-ever-after story for themselves.
>
> If the story doesn't unfold as hoped (and does it ever?), they will opt to question not the narrative but

themselves, for failing to become the heroines they should have been.[29]

ALL MY FAULT

In many cases, we suffer needlessly within a relationship, thinking the faults are all, always, our fault. In most cases, we suffer after the engagement is broken, because it *must* be our fault it ended. I imagine I will never have such a dissociative reaction to any experience as I had after my fiancé called off our wedding. I was shattered and completely relieved—at exactly the same time. How is that possible?

Traditionally, women are responsible for the health of relationships, while men are in charge of keeping families fed, clothed, and sheltered. Many families still pass down to their daughters the ideology that it's up to them to make partnerships work. We, in turn, tend to blame ourselves for relationships failing, and rush to change ourselves if we think it might make an engagement stick. I'd like you to be aware of all this still floating inside you, so you can shake it loose. As Heyn puts it, love is not earned through endless giving; sainthood is.[30]

WE'RE MAKING MARRIAGE BETTER

Pamela Paul told *People* magazine, "People I interviewed told me the best part of their marriage was either the wedding day or the divorce."[31] There's a long and storied history to the institution of marriage. With your broken engagement, you're helping to shape the institution into something better. On behalf of all women, I thank you.

RECOMMENDED READING

Your heart's broken, your mind's a mess. What do you need to read?

If you're

. . . sick of tulle and roses, I recommend Jacyln Geller's hilarious rip into weddings, *Here Comes the Bride: Women, Weddings and the Marriage Mystique.*

. . . looking for thought-provoking reading about making marriage right for you in light of the difficult history of the institution, I recommend Marilyn Yalom's *History of the Wife* and Dalma Heyn's *Marriage Shock: The Transformation of Women into Wives.*

. . . in need of reassurance that marriage can be a good thing, read Judith S. Wallerstein and Sandra Blakeslee's *The Good Marriage: How and Why Love Lasts.* Though it isn't their aim, the authors also give comfort to those of us who wonder if we could have made a shaky thing work after all. The stories of strong marriages show in bright relief the importance of a strong foundation.

. . . trying to lose yourself in some engrossing fiction for a few weeks, I recommend Margaret Mitchell's *Gone with the Wind.* From a "fast" Scarlett stealing kisses with her beaux to a demure Melanie constantly "hitching her top hoop a little higher" to hide her pregnancy, we've come a long way, baby.

Part 3

MOVING ON

Finding Comfort, Finding Strength

The fact that I called off my wedding one week out gave me strength. I faced my mother's hurt and disappointment, embarrassment, and leaving people with the impression that I was some kind of flighty weirdo to do something just for me. How great is that? I laugh sometimes to think about doing it. It was so tough to do, but such a good move. I am strong just for doing it.

—JESSICA

After unraveling the wedding plans, it's time to concentrate on the more important issue: you. Getting over any breakup is tough stuff, but getting over a broken engagement ratchets it up. This was someone you thought you'd spend your life with; it makes perfect sense to feel a deep sadness, anger, and lack of concentration. You'll feel generally off-kilter for a while, but there are things you can do—and shouldn't do—to speed the process of recovery.

MY STORY

I spent the first five weeks after my breakup sleeping on the couch of a good friend while I looked for a new place to live. I continued going to work every day, though I didn't do much more than busy work. In the evenings, I drank too much wine and cried. I never questioned what happened, but the emotions were incredibly painful, nonetheless. As modern couples do, we had already begun the process of melding our lives. We owned a home and shared his dog. We referred to each other as husband and wife to others; "fiancé" was such an awkward term, and using it necessitated a discussion of when the wedding would be and where we were in the planning.

In the early weeks after our breakup, I just wanted to go home. I still didn't want to marry him, but I wanted my life, my known reality, back. The alternative was too exhausting. I didn't want to be thirty-one and sleeping on a friend's couch, without a home.

Eventually, I found an apartment I could afford and moved in. I didn't have much in the way of belongings, so unpacking took little time. Feeling at home, in the apartment and in my own skin, took longer. Going to bed at night, alone and in a new place, was disconcerting. Waking in the middle of the night, I reached for him. In the morning, I was amazed it wasn't all a bad dream. Weren't we a team? What happened to our mantra "There is no more 'me and you.' There is only 'us.'"? Couldn't we have fixed anything? Deep down, I knew we had done the right thing. Postponing was, as he had said, just postponing the inevitable. I knew that although I loved him, I couldn't see my whole life with him. But the pain continued.

Then, all at once, I started to feel like I was getting a grip—producing more at work and having a great date with the hunky soldier/weekend moving man who supervised the move to my new apartment. Little did I know.

Losing My Grip

One morning, a colleague gave me a huge frying pan for my new apartment. After work, I stopped at the cleaners, picked up my dry cleaning, stashed it in the grocery bag that held the frying pan, and continued on my way.

I proceeded to the grocery store, bought dinner makings, and walked home.

At about ten that night, I realized I didn't have my dry cleaning. I went through my little apartment over and over, tearing open closet doors and searching in corners. I called the grocery store, but they hadn't seen my bag. I walked the four blocks back to the market, but the manager shrugged at my description. Suddenly overwhelmed, I walked the dark streets home and pulled out my cell phone. I punched in the number of my best friend. When she answered, I started crying. Why does he get the house? I demanded. Why doesn't he have to make a new home? Why, I wondered, senselessly, is his life untouched by this? I want to curl up with my dog, I cried. I want my life back. I sobbed, a fury I hadn't known I had in me boiling over, as she cooed meaningless comforts. I didn't want this. I wanted this. What did I want? Besides my dry cleaning back?

That was the low point, or, I should say, *a* low point (and my clothes are still out there, somewhere). There were also the nights I called friends at 2 A.M. because I couldn't sleep and I couldn't bear to be awake. Needless to say, my grip loosened. There was no way around it: I was suffering. I would continue to suffer intensely for about two months. Friends repeated their comforts over and over, until it felt like I was covered in a salve that my body refused to let soak in. I'd lose myself drifting at work. I needed that glass or two of wine after work. I didn't want to socialize; I didn't want to be alone.

Eventually, the roller coaster eased. The ride was slower, the dips (generally) more manageable. But they did come. Even months later, the Jewish New Year was rough. The rabbi spoke of new beginnings, and I was on board, but when I returned to my apartment, I once again was amazed and pained at the turn my life had taken. On September 11, as I watched footage of the planes destroying the World Trade Center over and over, I thought of him and hoped he was all right. As schools and businesses shut down across Washington, D.C., where I live, I watched for news of him, to know he was okay. I wanted, again, to be "home" with him, to know he was safe, that I was safe. That search for comfort hasn't ended.

NEEDING COMFORT, GETTING TERRIBLE ADVICE

We all start out life seeking comfort from our caregivers. According to the psychoanalytic model of comfort, infants rely entirely on their mothers—in particular, their mother's breast. Gradually, the infant learns to soothe herself and is able to fall asleep without nursing or being held. In the same way, when we suffer a painful loss, we initially need to depend on others to provide the comfort we crave. Gradually, we develop the ability to comfort ourselves.

Those who love you know that comfort is the best they can offer. But it's not so easy to give comfort to the woman who has broken an engagement. I love my friends and family, but I'm still amazed at some of the things people said to me. In the weeks after we called off the wedding, I found myself wondering, often: How can people be so stupid? In lieu of comfort, friends, family, and acquaintances offered up stunningly idiotic words. The myriad who said, "It's just cold feet; he'll be back," (huh? have you not heard a thing I'm saying?) and "you must have been embarrassed to call all those people" (embarrassment never crossed my mind; thanks for introducing it)— should have their mouths taped shut. At least temporarily.

I started a computer file I kindly named "Idiot Quotes" (hey, I wasn't sleeping anyway), and asked other Almost Brides to add to it. Let's all shake our heads together in disbelief:

Was it really that bad?

Did you give the ring back? Why?

In six months, you'll call me from Vegas and tell me you're married.

You should have made it work—he was nice and there aren't many nice ones out there.

I'd think the hardest thing would be realizing how wrong you were.

At least you have your career.

Didn't you lose a lot of money?

There's no one left—we're old and everyone's married.

I can't tell you it's going to get better. I'm not one of those people who believe it does.

What did you see in him?

Did you ignore the signs?

Put on some makeup and go out and meet someone new. (An Almost Bride's ex-future mother-in-law told her this one. On the day her fiancé broke the engagement.)

We had the same problem—but my husband really wanted to be with me, so it worked out.

When I heard, I called Jane and she said, "I can't believe
    it, I thought they were the perfect couple."
Was he cheating on you?
Were you cheating on him?
Is he gay?
Don't worry, there's someone else out there waiting for you.

I always wondered about that last one. À la that old *Mad
Magazine* gag "Snappy Answers to Stupid Questions," I
wanted to retort, "If you've got a crystal ball, why didn't you
warn me about what I was getting into?"

"IT COULD HAVE BEEN WORSE"

And then there are the well-meaning friends who pile on
with anecdotes of the most poisonous kind: The Girl Who
Had It Worse Than You. That poor girl. She's the one whose
fiancé called it off on the day of, in the synagogue, after his
mother fainted dead away. (This was supposed to be comforting to me because we called it off a full two weeks before
and no one passed out.) She's the one whose fiancé broke the
engagement once, they got back together, and then, on the
wedding day, he never showed up at the church. There are
the usual divorce stories: she was pregnant and he was
gay./She had a little boy, and one morning he got in the car
and left them. Turns out he had a whole other household
with someone else./He was controlling and mean and she left
him, but they have a child together, so he'll be in her life, still
controlling and mean, forever.

It gets so you can't believe that people continue to walk down the street and buy an ice cream cone, let alone keep dating. I was supposed to be comforted that the worst he did was call some of my friends and tell them he had dumped me and then not return all my belongings. Instead, it felt like, "this time he's calling my friends and keeping my wok; what's the next guy going to do?" I described it to one friend as jumping a wave only to worry that in the future I'd be nailed by a tsunami.

I felt like the world was raising its shirt to me and showing me its scars. "Jagged and dark aren't they?" the world said grimly. In those first few weeks, I couldn't hoist my shirt up fast enough, but it didn't do much for comfort or optimism. As Almost Bride Lilly said, "The horror stories of others didn't help me feel better. My situation wasn't changing just because someone else had a worse story."

As friends and family struggle to find comforting words, most Almost Brides find themselves subjected to such pronouncements as, "It's better now than after you married." Kelly acknowledges, "I'm sure it's awkward for them, too, to know what to say to someone who's just broken an engagement, but it wasn't anything I didn't already know."

Pella says, "My best friend laid a big ole 'I told you so' on me shortly after we split up. Quite frankly, she couldn't have chosen worse words to say."

SUFFERING AND SORRY SOLUTIONS

Almost Brides vary in the length and severity of their suffering after calling off their weddings. Amy says that she just felt relieved but was very worried for him, and Jodi says, "I wouldn't call it suffering; I called it rebuilding. I suffered while I was with him." At the other end of the spectrum, Karen says she was so depressed, she was suicidal for a while. Sandy, now engaged to someone else, says, "I believe I'm still suffering now, not in that I want to be with him, but [because] sometimes I miss him. More often than not, I feel guilt for leaving him and not 'fixing' his problems. It's about a year since I left him and I've only just sought counseling for it."

Grief

Almost Brides report difficulty eating, sleeping, and concentrating at work; all are hallmarks of grief (see Chapter Eight). Gretchen, who suffered for three years after her breakup, "lost twenty-eight pounds in about three weeks. I couldn't sleep. I was a wreck and suicidal." Stacey says, "The first week, I didn't sleep, didn't shower, didn't eat. Then my niece and nephew asked me if I was going to die. That snapped me out of it. After that, I ate everything in sight, had trouble sleeping unless I cried myself to sleep, and every night my dreams were full of him and our wedding."

Unsupportive People, Pouty Faces

The words and actions of others often contribute to that suffering. "Everyone thought I was crazy [for calling it off]," Amy says. "Everyone thought that I was making a huge mistake." Gretchen says, "The actions of his family beat me down a lot. After being with him for six years, I had become close to many of them and they just turned their backs on me." Lilly didn't appreciate pitying people who "looked at me with sad, pouty faces."

"Unsupportive people told me I was making a mistake," says Laura. "What do they know?"

Kelly's story is the extreme:

I couldn't function at work the first week. I couldn't seem to concentrate on anything and couldn't eat. There was that constant feeling like you've just been kicked in the stomach. That's the worst in the world. I'm sure everyone knows the feeling I'm talking about. One of my so-called best friends at the time came to my work one day when I couldn't function I was so upset. And when I told her I couldn't seem to move, she gave me this capsule and told me it was like a diet pill, and I would be able to work. Well, this was my best friend (I thought), and she knew I had *never* done drugs, didn't even *drink*. So I just took it. Looking back, it was stupid of me, but I wasn't in my right frame of mind, plus I trusted her. Turns out (I found out later), it was crystal meth. I didn't sleep for days and nearly went crazy with fatigue. Some friend, huh? She later confessed to me, because she "felt bad" for having done that. Um, yeah.

THANKS, BUT I CAN SELF-DESTRUCT ALL BY MYSELF

But the Almost Brides themselves aren't always blameless. You don't know what's going to give you comfort, so you're bound to make mistakes. Lilly "declared an entire weekend alone, but then realized I did need people." Others, because they feel like crap, try to escape the pain by attempting to numb themselves through drugs, alcohol, too much exercise, or promiscuity. Pella, for example, turned to drugs:

I was smoking pot every day and used it as a total escape route. I made horrible decisions in my personal life, I dated total losers, I was more promiscuous than I'd ever been. And my behavior contributed to losing two of my best friends forever.

I asked Almost Brides, What acts didn't give you comfort?

Agreeing to be fuck buddies with my ex—not saying *no*.   —KAREN

The effort I spent imagining resolving things with my ex and talking with him about where our relationship would go from here.   —DONNA

I had these fits of rage sometimes and often [spoke angrily of him] to our children, which I never should have done.   —GRETCHEN

I ate too much and stopped exercising.   —LISA

Being so weak I couldn't go running.   —LAURA

Calling him.   —BETSY

Thinking of him and wondering what I could have done—and there wasn't anything. I didn't deserve him cheating on me.   —AVERY

[Trying] to be friends immediately after the breakup. It was simply too soon.   —CLAUDIA

Comfort comes from all corners, if you go looking for it. Outside of yourself, you can get comfort from other people, food, drugs, sex, and exercise. While most of these can be healthy and constructive, they can all be destructive in excess. To determine if you're going overboard, it's helpful to compare your current behavior with your usual practices pre-breakup. Though it's not foolproof (after all, you might be unhealthy all the time), the comparison is important to evaluate whether there's been a significant change in your coping mechanisms. And if your means of comfort numb you instead, that's a definite sign you're going overboard. If you know you should cut back or cut out your bad behavior altogether and you just can't seem to do it, you should consider reaching out to a therapist or a program like Alcoholics Anonymous. Often, the most difficult step is actually admitting you need help. Please take a look at Chapter Nine if you see yourself here. Additional sources of help are listed in the Resources section.

GETTING THE COMFORT YOU NEED

The idea of getting the comfort you need begs the question, What can bring you comfort? For a short while there, nobody could say anything right to me. There is really no substitute for love and reassurance. When I asked her what helped, Andrea said it was when people told her, "You are a strong person and you will get through this" and "I am here if you need anything." Just as there is the decidedly *not* comforting Girl Who Had It Worse Than You, there's also the Envelope You in a Hug Girl who has been down this road. Can you see her there, at the end of the rutted dirt path? She's the one laughing and dancing. I'm that girl, and the women

I've surveyed are that girl, too. We're here to hug you and tell you you're on your way.

When the shock and intense pain gave way to paralyzing sadness, I called friends just to hear them promise me it would get better. When you are lost in the thicket, you need to hear the voices of people in the clearing. It will get better, and by "better" I don't mean "okay" or "livable"; I mean great. You will be back, and you will be better than you were. Every single one of the women I surveyed agreed with the statement "What does not kill you makes you stronger" and spoke of learning more about herself by going through a broken engagement than she could have imagined.

A woman who tends to be a listener and a caretaker but rarely opens up about herself can learn to share more about herself and grow from this experience. What you're suffering through now can lead to the development of richer relationships in the future, as well as a stronger inner self. I was afraid it wasn't going to get better and that I was going to feel like a failure forever. I wrote this book because it doesn't stay like that, and the difference in how I feel now, how well I know myself, and the confidence I have gained from this life-changing experience needs to be shouted from the rooftops.

We can't avoid life experience, nor would we want to. Think of spending an evening across the table from a world traveler, a great thinker, someone who has survived a war, witnessed a birth. Now think how much longer that evening would be if you spent it across the table from an eighteen-year-old college freshman who has experienced nothing but high school and a few keg parties. Which evening is going to go quicker and stay with you longer?

Getting the Comfort You Need from Others

In times of crisis, well-meaning friends and family members don't know what to do for you. They'll say, "Let me know what you need," both because they want to be there for you and because they don't know what, exactly, to offer you. Here's what you need from them:

- *Someone to listen, listen, listen.* Ask your friends and family to, just this once, not offer their take on the situation and tell you what a jerk they think he is. It helps to get the words out, and you'd really appreciate it if they'd sit quietly and listen to you vent.

- *Someone to listen at 2 A.M.* If a friend or family member says, "Call any-time," find out if she means it, and then take her up on it. Friends on the other coast are good in this situation. Others will be available during the workday or early in the morning. Find out their schedules so you're not venting to one person early, during work, and late at night. (You may also want to check out the chat boards on my Web site at www.theregoesthebride.com.)

- *Someone to check up on you.* The well-meaning but anxious friends aren't the ones for this. Find someone steady, whose voice by phone or e-mail makes you feel steady, and ask him to please check in.

- *Someone to get you out the door.* Some friends are better at doing than listening. In the face of grief and exhaustion, it's important to get moving. Find a friend to take a long walk, see a movie, or run errands with you.

- *Someone to sit at home with you.* Find the friend who'll order in pizza and watch *Seinfeld* with you. Preferably someone who has good taste in wine.

- *Someone who's been there.* Find the friend who has gone through a difficult breakup or divorce to let you know it's going to get better than this. Someday, you'll return the favor to another sufferer.

Getting Comfort from Others

Eventually, the words get through to you.

A lady I worked with had told me a few years before (about a totally unrelated subject), "You never see it when you're going through it, but when you look back on your life, you can always see God's hand." Meaning: God has a plan for you, whether you see it or not. And, of course, down the line you can always look back and be thankful things turned out the way they did. A paraphrase is part of the Desiderata, "Whether or not it is clear to you, no doubt the universe is unfolding as it should." Also, my mother, who never says anything bad about anyone, told me she had never liked his hair! For her, that is *way* catty!　　　　　　　　　　　—KELLY

I asked Almost Brides, What did others say or do that gave you comfort and strength?

When friends checked in to make sure I was okay, they knew whether to keep talking or just chat for a minute.　　　　　　　　　—LILLY

Having my cat near. Hearing my counselor tell me she loved me.

—KAREN

When my mother and I ran into a nosy person who said, "I thought you got married," my mother quickly responded, "No, she was smart." I don't know why, but that little comment from my mother helped me realize how right I was to call it off.　　　　　　　　　　　　—ERIN

My doctor gave me a few weeks' worth of Valium.　　　—BONNIE

When my sister said to me, "After you told me you were getting married, I said to myself, 'I have a year to convince her not to do this.'"

—BETSY

My male cousin said, "Never trust a guy who looks better in your bra than you do." —ROXY

Just being around my friends gave me some comfort. It reminded me that there were things to be thankful for. Also, the two girls I moved in with were down on men, too. So we had some good laughs and man-bashing sessions. That's not really fair to men in general, but at the time it made me feel better! —KELLY

A very close friend told me every day how cute I was and that my ex was a scuz for breaking my heart. —ANDREA

My father is my greatest confidant, and talking with him almost daily helped me through. My closest friends were also there to keep me busy and focused on the good things in life. —HILARY

Faith and good friends are what helped me the most. Some of my wonderful friends are happily married and assured me that if it is right, I will know. —LAURA

My best friend from college had gone through a similar breakup. Her relationship was different from mine, but she still broke off an okay relationship with a decent guy because she knew that they were not right for each other and could do better. Listening to her and hearing about her life afterwards gave me a lot of strength to do the same thing. She was the one who told me that he can be a great, wonderful guy and still not be the right one for me. It took me a long time to believe her, but I eventually realized she's right. —MATTIE

The biggest help was Al-Anon. I found a weekly meeting that I attended that truly changed my life and helped me to literally survive. —PELLA

Disney! My dad made arrangements for my older sister and me to go to Disney World for a week about a month after my fiancé and I broke up. It was important to me because it helped me realize that in all the suffering I was going through, I was still able to spend quality time with my sister and begin to build new memories and reestablish the relationships with my family. We spent the week visiting the parks and reminiscing about the family trips that we had taken years ago. She and I had a wonderful time, waking up at sunrise to get to the parks and staying up late into the night, enjoying park fireworks and parades. We spent the week sharing stories and desserts. She helped me to remember that there were other things that I had going for me, and she helped me realize that there was a world of possibilities for me to consider. —DONNA

Leaning Toward Our Infant Selves

During a trauma, we adults undergo an emotionally regressive period and, in a sense, lean toward our infant selves; during these difficult times, we depend more on others than we usually would. (If you are suffering horribly—like not sleeping or feeling terribly anxious or seriously depressed, you should talk to your doctor. There is only so much you have to bear. For information on getting more help, see Chapter Nine.)

But the bad times do go away; don't forget that. Almost Bride Hilary suffered terribly following the breakup of a long-term relationship prior to her broken engagement. "I learned so much from that experience," she says. "I learned that no matter how bad it gets, it *will* get better. That thought pulled me through this time."

Gradually, you'll depend on others and, possibly, prescription meds, less, and rely on yourself more. The timetable varies from woman to woman, depending, among other factors, on psychological strength, the circumstances of the breakup, and external resources.

Getting Comfort from Yourself

Time alone is necessary, but it's not enough. You need to try different ways of relaxing to see what works for you, as well as develop new interests. True self-comfort comes from doing for yourself whatever calms, soothes, and heals you, without resorting to artificial or numbing means. To do so, you'll need to build up your self-confidence, self esteem, and sense of independence—in some cases remembering the way it feels to be assured and free, and in others, developing it for the first time.

There are three aspects of this building. The first is developing independent, solitary activities that can be fulfilling, calming, and pleasurable.

The second is being patient with yourself as you ride your own personal roller coaster. Maybe your appetite is fine, but your concentration is shot. Maybe you want to be with people, but, when you are, you long to be alone. Maybe you felt great yesterday and keep crying today. No matter how your journey manifests itself, you must give yourself permission to feel bad. Many women suffer from guilt and inadequacy because they are sad, depressed, or overwhelmed, which only makes it harder to recover and move on.

Ask yourself:

- Do I feel ashamed or embarrassed for being so emotional?

- ◦ Do I keep saying to myself things like, "I shouldn't feel so terrible," "I shouldn't be so out of control," or "I should be able to handle this better"?
- ◦ Do I feel guilty about burdening my friends?

If you answer yes to any of these, you might not be permitting yourself to experience the necessary feelings involved in grief and loss. Consciously work on reminding yourself that this is an important part of the work of mourning (see Chapter Eight). This internal dialogue is also useful in developing our internal resources. If you find that you just can't take that close a look at your feelings of guilt and inadequacy, you may want to think about going deeper through therapy (see Chapter Nine).

Third, it's vital to take the time to care for yourself. Everything is easier with food in your belly and sleep logged. Everything is rougher without them.

I asked Almost Brides, What acts of yourself gave you comfort?

I went for a massage, sat at the beach, took a road trip, wrote and wrote and wrote in a journal.
—LILLY

I got into the girlie stuff for a while: took the time to have my nails done, got new clothes and jewelry—splurged on me with no guilt about it.
—ERIN

Buying my own house and distracting myself by furnishing it.
—KAREN

I read a lot of mysteries. They were easy to lose myself in.
—KELLY

Getting the Comfort You Need from Yourself

The weeks and months following a broken engagement are described by Almost Brides as a roller coaster. Here are some tips on making the ride less bumpy:

- *Cry, vent, get angry.* It's all normal and part of the process. If you find that you can't stop crying, can't sleep, and can't concentrate at work for longer than a few weeks, and talking to your friends and family isn't enough, consider meeting with a therapist. Almost Brides agree that it's wonderful to have a professional help you sort through your emotions. Almost Bride Laura calls therapy "a lifesaver."

- *Move around.* Take a walk. Moving clears your head, even if only for a little while. It's easier to sit and mope, but walking will increase your appetite, lower your stress level, and make it easier to sleep at night. If you can, continue your exercise habits. If you're just starting to exercise, start slow. You don't want to end up on the couch with any other muscles bruised in addition to your heart.

- *Take care of yourself.* In times of stress, it's easy to grab the quickest food or lose your appetite altogether. Taking care of your body—eating healthfully, getting sleep, exercising—goes a long way toward healing your mind and heart.

- *Let your friends and family take care of you.* Let someone else get dinner, choose a movie, or sit with you. Let people in. Your first instinct may be to shut everyone out, and sometimes you will, but it helps to have those who love you rally around.

- *Go through the motions.* Work may be the last thing you want to do, but it's helpful to have a place to go and a purpose in life. Get out the door in the morning and try to work. Now is the time to plow through those no-brainer redundant tasks you want to avoid when you're up to par. Do your filing. Organize your desk.

- *Be patient.* It simply stinks to feel crappy. Maybe you wanted this breakup, maybe you didn't, but you realize (as you should) that it's better this way. It's still a big loss and you're going to feel it. If you don't get the emotions out now, you'll suffer later. Get comfort from yourself and from others and cut yourself some slack. It will get better.

[After my second broken engagement,] I got a tattoo. At the time, it made me feel closer to him. I didn't feel the pain from the tattoo because the pain I felt from the breakup was so much more intense. My tattoo reminded me so much of my engagement ring and I even helped design the tattoo for that very reason. It is two dolphins; their tails are holding a heart and a teardrop is coming out of the heart.   —ELIZABETH

Doing what I wanted to do when I wanted to do it; I gave myself permission to treat myself.   —LAURA

I started back at college, which got me even more excited about my life. I loved it.   —AMY

I am not the most religious of people, but I have never prayed so much and so deeply in my entire life. I just prayed to God for guidance and strength.   —DEBBIE

I got busy: I worked full-time and I took some classes part-time.   —ABBY

Whenever I felt depressed or angry or humiliated, I would simply say to myself, "This, too, shall pass."   —CAROLYN

Went out with friends, met people, rediscovered myself, and redefined who I was.   —JESSICA

This is a little embarrassing, but listening to the Ace of Base song "Beautiful Life" really cheered me up. I think I wore out my tape!   —DANA

MACARONI AND CHEESE AND OTHER COMFORT FOOD

When you're talking comfort, there's got to be a discussion of comfort food. As Melissa Roth, author of *On the Loose*,[1] a documentary of single women, notes, nothing beats the restorative power of sushi. I discovered sushi late and have been trying my damnedest to make up for it ever since. I consider it my celebration food, and after my fiancé called off our wedding, I felt it only appropriate to celebrate. And as with all the best comfort foods, the sight of sushi gave me an appetite, and the taste made me forget my troubles for a bit. A month later, I got my American Express bill and, chastened, I cut back.

Some women can't bear to eat after their breakup. I asked those Almost Brides who did eat to share their favorite comfort foods:

Mac and cheese, cheese fries with ranch dressing.   —BETSY

Pour a cup of instant mashed potatoes into a bowl. Cover with a can of mushroom soup and a little water. Microwave for ninety seconds. Fast and filling.   —KAREN

Mashed potatoes and gravy.   —CLAUDIA

McDonald's french fries.

—CAROLYN

Stew in a crockpot.

—DEE DEE

Doritos and salsa.

—JILL

Mexican food, margaritas, rice crispy treats, cheesecake.   —JESSICA

Ice cream—almost any flavor and lots of it!   —MELISSA

On those long, lonely nights, fresh baked chocolate chip cookies. I suggest the Pillsbury dough roll. If you don't feel like baking, it's also great raw.

—LUCY

Chocolate is very helpful. One good mouthful of chocolate erases any tears that happen to be forming at the moment. Trust me.

—NAOMI

Takeout!

—LILLY

Cookbook author Joan Schwartz, otherwise known as my mother, offers this delicious, filling recipe by chef Keith Dresser from her popular book *Macaroni and Cheese: 52 Recipes from the Simple to the Sublime.*[2] It's comfort food at its best. Play some classical music, make a salad, stir the cheeses, and let the aroma fill your kitchen. Then light some candles, set the table, and treat yourself.

BAKED FOUR-CHEESE MACARONI

Enough for you and four friends—or you alone for the next few days (you lucky girl!):

8 tablespoons butter, plus extra for the baking dish

1 pound penne

4 cups whole milk

6 tablespoons flour

1^1/$_2$ teaspoons kosher salt

^{1}/$_4$ teaspoon cayenne pepper

2 cups (^{1}/$_2$ pound) grated sharp Cheddar cheese

2 cups (^{1}/$_2$ pound) grated Asiago cheese

2 cups (^{1}/$_2$ pound) grated fontina cheese

1 cup plain bread crumbs

^{1}/$_2$ cup (2 ounces) grated Parmesan cheese

2 tablespoons butter, melted

1 cup heavy cream

1. Preheat the oven to 350°F. Butter a 9 by 13-inch dish or 2^1/$_2$-half-quart casserole.

2. Bring 6 quarts of salted water to a boil. Add the pasta and cook, stirring occasionally, until al dente, for 10 to 12 minutes. Drain the pasta and rinse with cold water. Drain again and place in a large bowl.

3. In a medium saucepan over medium heat, bring the milk to a boil. Remove from the heat.

4. In a medium, heavy-bottomed saucepan over medium-high heat, melt the 8 tablespoons of butter. Reduce the

heat to low and whisk in the flour, cooking for 3 to 4 minutes. Be careful not to brown the mixture. Slowly add the hot milk, whisking constantly (constant whisking will ensure that there are no lumps). Add the salt and cayenne, raise the heat to medium, and simmer, stirring constantly, until the mixture has thickened, 8 to 10 minutes.

5. Remove from the heat and add 1 cup each of the grated Cheddar, Asiago, and fontina, whisking until the cheeses are melted. Pour the cheese sauce over the pasta, tossing to coat the pasta evenly.

6. Place half of the coated pasta in the buttered baking dish and distribute the remaining grated Cheddar, Asiago, and fontina over the top. Cover with the remaining pasta.

7. In a mixing bowl, toss together the bread crumbs, Parmesan, and melted butter. Pour the heavy cream over the pasta and evenly distribute the bread crumb mixture over the top. Bake on the middle shelf until the top is light brown and the mixture is bubbling, 30 to 35 minutes.

GAINING STRENGTH

As you become adept at comforting yourself, you'll find yourself getting stronger. Many women found that they could accelerate that process.

I asked Almost Brides, What acts of yourself gave you strength?

I bought my own house. I never thought I would buy a house without a man, but I did it! It was a great source of pride for me. It confirmed my independence and [showed] that I could get along without a man if I needed to. —DEE DEE

Getting up each day. Putting one more day behind me. —AVERY

The fact that I was able to call it off and not look back gave me so much strength. That was the greatest gift I had to give to myself. I was ready to take on the world. —ERIN

Spending more time at the rescue squad I volunteer with, saving others. —BETSY

I found strength in the fact that I wasn't wanting to call him back and try to work things out, although he had "dropped by" the new house to try to give me my mail in person. —KELLY

Making one of the toughest decisions I've ever had to make in my entire life, on my own, with everyone against me and telling me I was crazy. I had the strength and the courage to do it even though I had no idea what was going to happen to me. Also, being in school. I felt so empowered.

—AMY

I became very active in an on-line Huntington's Disease club and the local chapter of the Huntington's Disease Society of America. [This is a disease from which my mother suffers.] My involvement made me feel needed and strengthened my resolve. —HILARY

When I called everything off, he threw a fit on me and took my car keys and threw them into a nearby creek, grabbed my bag with my school books, then got in his own car and took off. I was stranded in the snow for hours until I could get hold of someone to take me home. The next night I told him to meet me at school to return my books, and when he tried to work things out again and I told him no, he got very angry again and gave me a black eye. I had him arrested, and that was the last time I ever saw him.

Now, while we were together, he made me a scrapbook of pictures and things from our relationship. When I was ready to fully move on and let go of that part of my past, I took that scrapbook to the creek where he threw my keys, and threw in the scrapbook. Then I drove up to my school and said a little prayer in the parking lot where he hit me. Those actions of my own gave me such immense strength, the strength I needed to move on.   —PELLA

I went back to school and made something of my life.   —GRETCHEN

I felt very strong for standing up to someone who was potentially life-threatening. Going to work each day gave me strength, even though I spent a lot of time crying in the bathroom.   —SANDY

ON THE REBOUND

Look at you, standing so strong, with your full stomach! Ready to start thinking about the next step? That's dating, and if the thought makes you cringe, I'd venture to guess you're not quite ready yet. Hey, that's okay. Almost Brides differ on jumping back into the social fray. Many surveyed found that the man they would eventually marry was right there all the time (see Chapter Ten for more on moving on). But for most of us, any dating we'll be doing in the weeks and months after calling off our weddings won't be with marriage in mind. Bluntly, we're going to be on the rebound. And Almost Brides are split on the helpfulness of rebounds. Robin is all for them. "Dating other people, as bad as it sounds, made me realize that he wasn't The One. There were so many other people who intrigued me and made me see how flawed our relationship had been," she says.

I asked Almost Brides, How long did you wait before delving into the dating world again?

I had a couple of dates in the year after the engagement broke up. A couple of years later, I was in a relationship for maybe eight months but couldn't open up. I don't know if it wasn't the right guy or if I was still keeping my heart under lock and key. Either way, it never got serious. I stayed a hermit (relationship-wise) a *long,* long time. It was four years after calling it off that I met Eli and allowed myself to love someone again.   —KELLY

Two months. Because I am weak, or was. A good-looking guy asked me out, so of course I said yes.   —KAREN

About two months after breaking up with my fiancé, I met my current boyfriend. I honestly wasn't looking, but he was too good to pass up. My frame of mind is more of a—it's his loss, not mine. And why mourn something that wasn't meant to be? At least that is what I try to think; it helps me get through the harder days.   —LISA

Waited two weeks after the final breakup. Not sure why. It was definitely too soon, but I needed to feel loved.   —GRETCHEN

About a year or so. The first guy I dated was actually my current fiancé's best friend at the time. It was too soon, though. It was almost like I was trying to prove something to myself. I had several stupid relationships with guys in bars. My fiancé is the first serious boyfriend I've had since calling it off, and came four years later, and that's the one that stuck.   —PELLA

Three weeks. I fell for a friend immediately. Big mistake.   —LAURA

Eight months. For a long time, I could not conceive of being with anyone but him and really didn't even want to. I probably only started to date at the beginning because others told me I had to. And then, of course, problems actually finding men to date arose.   —TAMARA

Two years. I was frightened. My only experience [had been] a bad one. I even had some bad ones, once I started dating again, but I got back on the horse, and thank God I did.   —SUSAN

I really didn't wait at all. I was with my fiancé for six years. The relationship was really over long before I finally called it off. Emotionally I was out of the relationship years before it was over and I was ready to move on.
     —ERIN

Two months or so. I'm not sure if I waited on purpose; it just worked out that way. I met someone and started dating. [Not long after,] I met my current fiancé. I was struggling with the "there she goes again" that I figured everyone was saying. So [we] kept the details of our relationship to ourselves.   —HILARY

I waited only a few months. Why? Because I was stupid. I should have waited longer, because I delved right into another bad relationship.
     —DANA

I waited only about a week. It was right for me. I'm very much a "no-nonsense" kind of person. If he didn't want to be with me, then I would move on as well.   —MELISSA

About one and a half years. I needed to get to know myself first before I got into another bad relationship.   —LUCY

Relationship guru John Gray, author of the *Men Are from Mars, Women Are from Venus* series, suggests "dating around but not sleeping around."[3] Almost Bride Kate agrees. "I found a complete change of scenery the best cure for me, so I moved to England for six months," she says. "I threw myself into my third term of law school and very casually dated (no intimacy!) a few different people. I didn't trust my feelings, and I didn't know when I would be able to trust them again, so I just took things one day at a time."

Getting What You Need from Dating

Everybody's timetable is different. As with any breakup you've gone through, there isn't a correct formula to follow, and many variables affect the speed and ease of your emotional recovery. One is just luck: maybe you'll call a good guy friend to cry and find yourself laughing instead, and think, hmmm . . . (though I still counsel you to take your time).

Another variable to consider are those underlying psychological factors that may have kept you tethered to the relationship longer than you should have been. While it cannot be overstated that breaking an engagement is an act of strength, you should take this opportunity to ask yourself:

- Do I often stay in a relationship longer than I feel good in it?
- Do I have trouble asserting myself to my partners or telling my partners what I need?
- Do I have a pattern of staying in negative or undesirable relationships and not being able to do anything about it?

- ○ Do I have a habit of staying in negative or undesirable relationships and not recognizing them for what they are until I'm out of them?

"Yes" answers show certain patterns that keep you from getting the most out of relationships and may keep you from recovering from the breakup of your engagement in a timely manner. Now is the time to explore your patterns, either on your own or with the help of a therapist.

MY STORY

Personally, getting off the couch and pushing myself to rebound definitely helped my recovery from calling it off. Agreeing to a date with the soldier/moving man I referred to earlier in this chapter was one of the smarter things I did as I maneuvered my way back to normalcy.

He was tall, built, sweet, and gorgeous. Also, eight years younger. We got to e-mailing in the days after he moved me in, and when he suggested dinner, I asked if he was up for sushi (of course). Being from Deep Midwest, population five thousand, he'd never had sushi. He didn't much like it, but he loved my stories of "life in the big city" (New York) and cracked me up with tales of life in the armed forces. After dinner and much wine, we went to a pool hall, where we showed off our lousy pool skills, and I refused to tell him how old I was. At the end of the evening, despite my friends' urgings to be sure to bring him home, I left him at the door. He kissed my hand and thanked me for my company. Me! An "old" woman, with her life still in boxes and her head a mess. He's gone off to the Middle East since, but we've kept up our friendship. I'm sure he has no idea what he did for my self-confidence in those early days.

But it wasn't as if I was off and running after that one date (and for all I know, he thought he was just having sushi with a nice woman). After we had dinner, I retreated into myself for the rest of the summer, getting back to me. Then, in October, I attended a costume Halloween party, determined to find a date. I spent the night dancing with Danny, a tall, cute runner. On our first date, I declared that I was just out of an engagement and wasn't looking for a serious relationship. "If you're looking for someone to marry," I told him, "keep looking."

It felt freeing to say what I needed out loud. He wasn't too happy about it, and my rebound relationship lasted just a month. Which was perfect for me. After those Saturday nights of movies, dinners, and laughter, I felt ready to reenter the dating world and began to allow friends to set me up on blind dates. I knew I was feeling better when I could endure the difficult ones, enjoy myself at the fun-but-no-chemistry ones, and return home emotionally in one piece.

Healthy Versus Unhealthy Dating

Healthy dating can boost your self-esteem and remind you that you are desirable and that there are other men out there. Unhealthy dating can be a way of shifting your dependency from one guy to another or just trying to avoid the pain of loss by merely replacing your fiancé. Distinguishing between the two is largely intuitive; as with all aspects of this journey, it's important to stay clear on what you need and why. If you are enjoying meeting new men and not getting into a relationship in which your whole interest is focused on someone new, you're in good shape. If you find yourself preoccupied with someone else or are centering your life around another person soon after calling off your engagement, chances are you're moving too fast.

When it comes to recovering, you often have to feel worse before you can feel better. If you find that you are throwing yourself into dating and are clinging to one man or sleeping with many, you're not letting yourself go through mourning. Sure, it would be great to put the breakup behind you and just move on, but if you rebound too fast or too hard, there's a good chance you won't be able to realistically evaluate whether this relationship is good for you or just a shifting of dependence. Worse, you run the risk of repeating old patterns.

Furthermore, those who don't heal from one major loss or trauma inevitably bring the emotions they are repressing into all aspects of their life. Unresolved baggage will get too heavy to carry. As stated earlier, it's pretty likely that you won't know if the new guy is good for you or just a handy example to yourself that you're doing fine and moving forward. It's also crucial to give yourself a chance to heal so that the issues don't dog you in your next relationship. And, finally, pursuing gratification and comfort from a new relationship too soon can leave you believing that you need to be in a relationship in order to feel good. You're at risk of losing a sense of yourself as a confident, separate, strong individual. And that sense of strength is priceless.

STUCK IN YOUR PAIN

If you've suffered an early life loss—like the death of a parent or sibling—or have parental issues from your childhood and have not had the opportunity to fully explore and come to terms with them, you may have a more difficult time dealing with your broken engagement. If you have suffered such a loss and find yourself stuck in your pain, I suggest you talk to a professional.

Being "stuck" is more than being sad, angry, or even, at times, overwhelmed. The question to face is: How much are your emotions affecting the rest of your life, and for how long? Sadness and short-term depression at this time are reactions to the loss you've just experienced, and the emotions those bring are generally clear: sadness, anger, and so forth. Clinical depression is less specific: if what you are feeling is not deep sadness or feelings of loss (although your feelings may have begun that way) but rather a feeling of lethargy and a lack of interest in anything, you may be suffering from clinical depression. Chapter Nine includes the indicators of clinical depression.

YOU'RE IN THE SWAMP RIGHT NOW

Sure, sure, you say. But I just want to feel better!

You will, I promise. We all promise. I told Almost Brides: a woman who has just called off her wedding is standing here, in front of you. Then I asked them, what do you tell her?

Sit down and talk about it. Get it all out: cry, scream, do whatever you feel like doing. Don't put on a brave face for others. —FIONA

As much as it hurts right now, this doesn't compare to the hurt you might have felt had you gotten into the wrong marriage. The hurt will go away, I promise. —TERI

Be patient with yourself; allow yourself time to heal. Feed your self-respect and dignity. —PELLA

Understand that other people react based on their own experiences and views. Try to be cognizant of that and it will drive you crazy less.
—LILLY

Even though it feels like your life has been ruined, you've actually just been given an amazing opportunity—the opportunity to find your own identity again. You are going to come out on the other side of this a stronger, smarter, and much happier person. —SOPHIE

If you don't get married, it's not the end of the world. The end of the world is losing your self—and your self-respect. If he wants to change you, or you want to change him, get out now. It ain't going to happen. Or, if it does, it won't change anything that really matters. Someone who wants you to change really wants to control you. Control types don't make great parents—or husbands. They make great jailers. —ROXY

Take it one day at a time and realize how much better things are because he's gone. Things do happen for a reason. If you don't see it now, you will. I would also recommend counseling. —AVERY

You will get through this. Life is a rocky road with lots of twists and turns. You just have to stay on the road. —ELIZABETH

If this was not the right relationship for you, you have just done the most courageous thing you could have done. You just need to devote some time and attention to taking care of yourself and healing. The right relationship will come along when you are actually ready for it. —ELLY

Trust yourself to make good decisions. Don't look back. You will get past this and still have a wonderful life. —ABBY

Learn who you are on your own. Explore parts of you that you doubt now, decide where you want to go from here, and move forward. And surround yourself with love—from people who love you and from yourself.

—GRETCHEN

Stay away from your ex. —KAREN

Be strong. Don't let anyone treat you like you are the bad guy or make you feel guilty for any reason. —AMY

Many people wish they were in your shoes right now. —LAURA

No amount of effort is going to make a relationship work if it's not meant to be. In my case, it wasn't meant to be at all, but I didn't want to see it, so I tried and tried. Then when it didn't work, I blamed myself. Do not take all the responsibility on yourself. When something ends, it's because it wasn't meant to be. You can't blame yourself for that. You don't have that kind of power. Most importantly, don't give up on love. —SAMANTHA

It takes time to heal. That's all there is to it. I look back four years now, and it was the best decision I could have ever made. —LYNN

I respect and admire you. —JILL

You're stuck in the middle of a big, nasty, mucky swamp right now, and it's tough and stinky and depressing, but the only way out of it is just to keep going until you're out. The middle is the deepest, hardest part, but the closer you get to the "shore," the easier it gets, but you'll never get there just sitting in it! I mean, you have to grieve, but after a while, you've got to work your way toward brighter days, too! And there *are* brighter days waiting for you!

—KELLY

Chapter

8

Is It Grief When I Wish He Were Dead?

Understanding Grief, Anger, and All the Other Emotions

I tried to pretend it hadn't happened. That probably was the worst thing I could do. It took me a long time to get past it. It was years before I allowed myself to mourn it. I kept telling myself I was happy it was over and there was no reason to mourn it.

—ABBY

MY STORY

When I returned to Washington after a week with my family, I phoned an acquaintance who had called off her wedding three months before me. A month or two earlier, I had run into her on the bus and was acutely aware that she, radiating a peace I hadn't possessed in too long, was a hell of a lot happier than I was. Now we met for lunch in the park in front of my office, and as she pulled off the top of her Tupperware container, she commented that it was nice to eat with someone, since she still had trouble getting herself to eat. I nodded while thinking, *I* plan to be *fully* healed in three months.

She told me her story and described the man she had begun to date (now, a year later, they're happily engaged). Then she said something that stayed with me for a long time: "Look for books on grief."

Grief? How could this be grief? We didn't have a dead body, though I admitted to fleeting thoughts of how this would have been easier if we did. She shook her head firmly: this was grief. A different kind maybe, but there weren't any books for our situation.

I thought for a long while that she was deluded. What I was suffering from had many names—sadness, relief, depression, fatigue, confusion, but I doubted they added up to grief.

I was wrong. Now that I am looking back on it from a distance, I recognize the feelings for what they were and the passage beyond them as nothing short of a journey out of grief.

GRIEF AND MOURNING

When someone dies, we grieve. We also grieve—and mourn and experience bereavement and possibly feelings of abandonment—when we break an engagement. If you believe (as I do) that there must be a death to experience grief, you can think of it this way: what has died and must be "gotten over" is our vision of the future.

What is the difference between grief and mourning? *Grief* is the emotion of deep sorrow and longing to have your loved one back. *Mourning* refers to the outward expression of grief—that is, any action or ritual that helps us cope with our loss. Mourning is influenced by the culture in which we grew up, while grief is more instinctive.[1]

Bereavement refers to the feeling of having to do without someone we feel a need for. The Almost Bride is bereaved because she is deprived of the man she loved—or loves—and depended on.[2]

Abandonment means experiencing separation as a desertion; that person you needed up and left you. In death, feeling abandoned by someone may be irrational—after all, he couldn't help going, but it can be a very powerful feeling. Similarly, if *you* are the one who broke your engagement or, as in my case, you were pushing for it or (when rational) are fully aware that it needed to happen, feeling abandoned can strike you as downright odd. It may help to realize that feelings of abandonment now can be a reliving of a much earlier experience (possibly back to infancy) of perceiving a separation as a kind of desertion.[3]

THE FIVE STAGES OF DEATH AND DYING

Many of our ideas about dealing with grief are based on the experience of facing death: our own and the death of our loved ones. One of the most famous psychological studies was conducted by Dr. Elisabeth Kübler-Ross in 1969.[4] Her work with dying patients led to the development of five stages of dealing with death and dying:

1. *Denial and isolation.* This involves a psychological mechanism called "splitting": one part of the mind acknowledges the loss, while the other denies it.
2. *Anger.*
3. *Bargaining.* In this stage we make a kind of "psychological deal" with God or some greater being or force in an effort to reverse fate, thinking that if we had done something differently, things would have worked out better.
4. *Depression.*
5. *Acceptance.* In Kübler-Ross's study, the fifth stage of acceptance is reached when a dying person has spent

time working through the four previous stages. In this stage the person is neither angry nor depressed. Kübler-Ross talks about this not being a happy stage but rather a time almost "void of feelings . . . as if the pain had gone, the struggle is over."[5]

Kübler-Ross dealt with death and dying, but the stages apply to your situation, too, and acceptance following any loss is the final goal of the grieving process. It is the stage in which we acknowledge the situation for what it is, or accept the loss and move on with our lives.[6]

Also associated with acceptance is the realization that we don't have control over many aspects of our lives, but can use this experience to develop ourselves further. We can reevaluate our lives, learn from this experience of loss, and reinvest in ourselves and our futures.[7]

In Kübler-Ross's theory of grieving, still widely accepted more than thirty years later, the mourner moves through each of the first four states before finally accepting her loss. In the breakup of a relationship (be it a separation, divorce, or broken engagement), the mourning process takes a different course, since the significant other is still around. Since he's available for interaction, as well as legal or material negotiations, this interaction becomes part of the grief work. The chief difference between death and other types of separation is the ability to return for a real-world look at the other person. You are lucky your fiancé didn't die, for more than the macabre reasons. Since he's still here, you are pretty well prevented from idealizing him and building him into a fantasy that never was. If he's still out there sleeping with his ex-wife, it's more difficult to think, "Well, maybe it was just that one time. He loves me so much . . ."

But it is important to remember that the process of grieving is fluid; we go in and out of different stages, without set rules or time limits. So (unfortunately), reaching acceptance does not necessarily mean that we are finished grieving.

MAJOR PHASES OF GRIEF

Another way to organize our thinking about the process of mourning is to divide it into two major phases:

1. *Crisis grief,* which incorporates Kübler-Ross's five stages and basically deals with the task of accepting or dealing with the reality of the loss.
2. *"The work of mourning,"* a phrase coined by Sigmund Freud in 1917,[8] which describes the internal and external adjustments made after a loss. This is all part of the subtle and complex emotional work required in "letting go." (See Charting Your Emotional Recovery below.)

The course of mourning depends on preparation for the loss, the character of the lost relationship, the mourner's psychological strength, and the mourner's capacity to grieve or confront the many emotional aspects of her loss.

CHARTING YOUR EMOTIONAL RECOVERY

The emotional recovery of a broken engagement involves a mixture of intense emotions and experiences that may include any or all—or none, if you're really lucky—of these, in any order:

- Mourning/grief over the loss
- Anger
- Anxiety/panic
- Depression
- Disappointment
- Frustration
- Guilt
- Shame
- Feelings of rejection, low self-esteem

(Before you freak out, let me assure you that *they pass,* and we're here to help you get through them. Plus, you get the joy of experiencing some of them simultaneously, so you won't still be feeling some of these eight, ten years from now.)

The most basic psychological theories that underlie all of these reactions have to do with separation issues—in particular, separation anxiety. The ability to handle life's transitions is shaped by our first interactions with a mother or caretaker. If our early interactions were basically constant, trusting, and loving, we can draw on this foundation in the face of change. We grow by giving up: we give up the breast to progress to drinking from a cup; we give up being carried to progress to walking on our own.

You may be stumbling now, but you will give up this relationship and progress to a stronger you.

EMOTIONAL REACTIONS TO LOSS

Understanding these emotions can help you recognize your feelings and get through this tough time. If you feel you need more help, you may wish to consider therapy. I discuss this further in the next chapter.

Grief

Babies depend on their attachment to mother (or the mother figure) in order to survive. They cry out in grief and terror when separated from her. Even though the separation is usually temporary, it leads to powerful emotions that don't end with infancy. Different grief patterns between individuals can be identified in the second or third year of life. As we grow, we carry the same feelings and behaviors we experienced from infancy as well as others that develop over the years.[9]

Anger

When children are allowed to express their emotions, they can usually get over these feelings pretty quickly. However, when they're told to deny the existence of those feelings, the stage is set for later emotional difficulties. Repressing our emotions requires more energy than expressing them and can lead to deep-seated resentment and bitterness, jealousy, even hate. If as children we can understand, express, and deal with our emotions in a constructive way, the above reactions won't have a chance to take over.[10]

Anxiety and Panic

Common reactions after loss are anxiety and moments of panic. Anxiety is a state of nervousness and apprehension, signaling some kind of danger. After a significant loss, the danger may be associated with worry about our future in a general or more specific sort of way. Anxiety may be accompanied by sudden, brief, and intense panicky feelings. We understand that it's the loss itself that makes us anxious and panicky. And in serving as a kind of warning signal, these feelings can help mobilize us to take steps to protect ourselves in the future. This is different from the experience of anxiety and panic suffered by someone with an anxiety disorder, which is not correlated with a specific cause and does not serve a purpose.[11]

Sometimes anxiety and panic can lead to a state known as a panic attack. Symptoms of panic attacks include chest discomfort, choking or smothering sensations, faintness, fear of imminent death or loss of control, feelings of unreality, heart palpitations, nausea, abdominal distress, sweating, shortness of breath, shaking, and tingling sensations.[12] Panic attacks in grieving individuals are often triggered by the stress of grief and are possibly more likely to occur if the sufferer does not acknowledge or express her feelings more directly.

If you believe you are suffering from panic attacks, it's important to see a doctor to rule out the possibility that the feelings you're experiencing aren't a side effect of a medicine you're taking or the symptoms of another condition. A doctor can also prescribe antianxiety medication or recommend you get some behavioral therapy to stop the attack in its tracks.

It's also important for you to realize that though it may feel like it, panic attacks *won't* kill you. You can ride the wave and know that the feeling will gradually diminish. If you're driving, pull over during a panic attack. You'll feel out of control, but that control will return.

Depression

It is natural to feel saddened or down after a loss. The difference between the normal experience of depression after a loss and different types of clinical depression lies in the intensity and duration of the experience of "feeling depressed." (I go into this in more detail in the next chapter.)

Disappointment and Frustration

Both of these powerful emotions often accompany, and are sometimes difficult to distinguish from, depression. Disappointment can represent a transition point in grief as you shift from anger. Frustration refers to the experience of feeling stuck or thwarted in your attempts to resolve a conflict or accomplish a task over an extended period of time.[13]

Guilt

This feeling comes from inside you (in contrast to shame, which is externally generated) and contains remorse, sadness, and anger directed at yourself.[14] In a healthy grieving process, a woman can learn to forgive herself and learn from her mistakes. As strange as it may seem, you can feel guilty, regardless of who initiated the breakup. But when the guilt persists for an extended period of time and continues to be felt intensely, it may be a sign of clinical depression. (See Chapter Nine for more on this.)

Shame

As stated earlier, shame is triggered by others—their words, actions, even body language.[15] The message you get from others is a judgmental one: you *shouldn't* feel the way you do, you *shouldn't* behave the way you are. The general idea is that it's somehow wrong to feel grief or go through a mourning process—particularly if it inconveniences or makes others uncomfortable. Of course, individuals vary in the degree to which they are susceptible to others' attitudes and comments. This vulnerability is directly related to the person's level of self-esteem—the next and last category of reactions to be discussed in this chapter.

FEELINGS OF REJECTION
AND LOW SELF-ESTEEM

The concept of low self-esteem is one of those labels that has been so overused it's in danger of becoming almost meaningless. But it refers to a woman's basic attitude toward herself and has a tremendous impact on all areas of her life. When the other person breaks off a relationship, particularly something as significant as an engagement, it is usually experienced as a rejection—the sense of being discarded and feeling inadequate and undesirable. This can be felt even if the rejected woman was beginning to question her own feelings of interest in her partner. Consequently, if she is also quite insecure and dependent on others' interest in her—particularly the man she is about to marry, her reaction can be one of devastation—feeling greatly diminished in importance and even worthless. If these kinds of feelings persist (as with the other emotions discussed here) beyond the early weeks following a breakup, they may be a sign of more serious emotional problems that need to be clinically treated.

Chapter 9

Getting More Help

When to See Your Doctor or a Therapist

❀ ❀ ❀

I threw myself into my work because I didn't want to go home. I didn't sleep without prescription help. I didn't eat (lost twenty-five pounds). I withdrew from my friends and family because I was more embarrassed than anything else. I drank a lot and generally felt like a failure. When I wasn't working, I was drinking, lying in bed crying. —BONNIE

MY STORY

Shortly before the breakup, I sought professional help. I didn't get what I needed from my therapist, so when Mark and I split up, I found a different one, and this time it all came together. I started out just wanting to feel better and I ended up delving into why I got so close to doing something I hadn't wanted to do. In my case, and in those of many of the Almost Brides I interviewed, taking the time to focus on myself with the help of a professional at this difficult time was well worth the expense.

SOMETIMES YOU NEED MORE

Almost Bride Kelly likens recovery from a broken engagement to walking through a swamp, but what if you're trudging and trudging and you still can't get to shore?

I know I've been a broken record on this but it bears repeating: what you're going through absolutely sucks, but it gets better. Sometimes all you need is time and the support of loved ones, and sometimes you need more. This chapter will help you identify when and how to seek professional help, understand different types of depression, and become informed about antidepressant medication.

WHAT IS DEPRESSION?

The National Institute of Mental Health explains that a depressive disorder is

> an illness that involves the body, mood, and thoughts. It affects the way one eats and sleeps, the way a person feels about oneself, and the way one thinks about things. A depressive disorder is not the same as a passing blue mood. It is not a sign of personal weakness or a condition that can be willed or wished away. People with a depressive illness cannot merely "pull themselves together" and get better. Without treatment, symptoms can last for weeks, months, or years. Appropriate treatment, however, can help most people who suffer from depression.[1]

Symptoms of Depression

The following are symptoms of depression:

- General feelings of sadness
- Total loss of interest and pleasure in things that have previously pleased you
- Feelings of apathy
- A sense of worthlessness
- Inappropriate guilt—the feeling that it's all your fault, even though rationally and intellectually you realize that you shouldn't take the blame
- Feelings of hopelessness. Hopelessness is a timeless feeling. One of the classic features of depression is

that you can't imagine a point in the future when you won't feel this way.

- Crying spells
- Eating disturbances—either loss of appetite or overeating (compulsive eating/binging)
- Sleep disturbances—chronic insomnia or excessive sleeping, and chronic fatigue in either case
- Increased anger and resentment. In some people, this feeling leads to tantrums—out-of-control screaming and attacking, be it verbally or physically directed toward the person who caused the pain or toward whomever happens to be around. Others will intermittently overreact in an overtly aggressive way to everyday situations. Still others will contain most of their angry, aggressive feelings and thoughts.
- Reduced libido, sometimes resulting in no sexual interest at all
- Difficulty concentrating, with distraction occurring easily
- Increased anxiety and the possible onset of panic attacks or the development of phobias
- Restlessness—difficulty sitting still
- Flattened affect—slow body movements and speech
- Suicidal thoughts[2]

Three Classifications of Depression

In discussing the different classifications of depression, I refer to the *Diagnostic and Statistical Manual of Mental Disorders*

(DSM-IV, 4th ed.), which provides the currently accepted diagnostic terms and codes used nationally in the mental health field.

Major Depressive Disorder. In a major depressive disorder, a person suffers from symptoms of depression for most of the day, nearly every day, for a period of at least two weeks. Specific symptoms can vary from one woman to another (and, obviously, from one man to another, but I'm sticking to women here, as it's my assumption that most readers of this book are women), but there are general feelings of sadness and a total loss of pleasure in things that have previously pleased her. If this diagnosis is followed by "Single Episode," it means that this is the first time a depression of this type has been experienced.[3]

Dysthymic Disorder. In this depression, a woman has been chronically depressed, but in a milder way, for a longer period of time. According to the DSM-IV, "the essential feature of Dysthymic Disorder is a chronically depressed mood that occurs for most of the day more days than not for at least two years."[4] In a dysthymic disorder, a woman feels at least two of the symptoms included in the preceding list, in combination with a generally sad or "down in the dumps" mood.[5]

Adjustment Disorder with Depressed Mood or Adjustment Disorder with Mixed Anxiety and Depressed Mood. This diagnostic classification is especially pertinent to us. According to DSM-IV, "the essential feature of an Adjustment Disorder is the development of clinically significant emotional or behavioral symptoms in response to an identifiable psychosocial stressor or stressors. The symptoms must develop within three months after the onset of the stressor(s). The clinical significance of the reaction is indicated either by marked distress that is in excess of what would be expected given the nature of the stressor, or by significant impairment in social or occupational (academic) functioning."[6]

The key to the diagnosis of an adjustment disorder (rather than a major depressive disorder or a dysthymic disorder) has to do with identifying the stressor or stressors. An adjustment disorder is diagnosed when a woman's emotional state exceeds some normal range of expected reaction (which is called grief or mourning) and strays into some "excess" of that range, either in the amount of time the symptoms last or in the acuteness of her symptoms.

It is also possible to have a long-term dysthymic disorder and suddenly experience a major depression. In fact, DSM-IV estimates that each year approximately 10 percent of individuals with dysthymic disorder will go on to have a first major depressive episode.[7] And a significant loss—like the breakup of an engagement—may very well trigger a major depression in someone who has already been suffering from a low-level dysthymic disorder.

GETTING HELP

You've made up your mind that you want to find help to get through. Here's how to go about it:

Start with Your Physician

If you are confused about whether you're experiencing depression or going through a normal period of mourning, it is probably best to begin by seeing your primary care physician. Provide your doctor with a brief family history and request a medical workup to rule out such conditions as an underactive thyroid, mononucleosis, anemia, diabetes, adrenal insufficiency, and hepatitis.[8] It's also important to look at any prescription medications you are taking, since some drugs can have depressive side effects. Some common ones include birth control pills, benzodiazepines, some phenothiazines, clonidine, cortisone-like steroids, and digitalis. Be sure to tell your doctor about any vitamins, herbal medicines, diet supplements, and, of course, mood-altering substances you take regularly.

Once she has ruled out a medical condition or some possible drug-induced state of depression, let her know that you're going to consult with a mental health professional. (It's always a good idea to keep your primary physician in the loop.)

Who to Talk To

You've got a few choices here. Those trained to treat clinical depression are the following professionals:

○ *The psychiatrist.* Of these professionals, only psychiatrists have a medical degree. They have completed an internship and a psychiatric residency (for a total of eight years, on average) and are allowed to prescribe medication. (Psychiatrists won't necessarily suggest medication and you are under no obligation to agree to medication if you see a psychiatrist.) If you choose one of the other professionals mentioned below, and, together, you decide to try medication, you two will need to consult with a psychiatrist or your physician to get that prescription. Choosing to see a psychologist or other non-prescribing therapist and working in consultation with a psychiatrist isn't a problem; many people choose to go this route.

○ *The psychologist.* Instead of an M.D., psychologists have completed a Ph.D. in clinical psychology. This training takes three years of graduate work and a one-year internship. A clinical psychologist's training includes psychological testing and assessment, which can be helpful in making differential diagnoses as well as arriving at appropriate treatment plans.

○ *The clinical social worker.* This professional has obtained a master's degree in clinical social work (M.S.W.). Formal training is two years of graduate work (including the internship). In addition, independent clinical social work practitioners must be licensed; to receive the title of L.C.S.W., social workers must also have one year of supervised clinical practice after receiving their M.S.W. degree. This academic training develops expertise in family and interpersonal relationships.

○ *The counselor.* Counselors have a variety of backgrounds. Most have a master's degree in counseling from either a school of education or a psychology department. Some are ministers or rabbis who may have training or experience in counseling. Those who are licensed professional counselors have completed a state-approved training program; this generally requires two years of graduate education, which includes some intern work.

HOW TO CHOOSE THE RIGHT THERAPIST

To choose the right therapist for you, be sure to follow these criteria:

- He or she must be licensed to practice in his or her field in the state.
- Get a recommendation or referral from someone you know and respect: your primary care physician, gynecologist, or a friend or family member. If you can't get a personal recommendation, get in touch with one of the professional associations listed in Find Help Fast, in the Resources section at the end of this book, for a referral. If your health insurance company has its own network of mental health providers, you may have to choose somebody from that network in order to be fully covered.
- It is crucial that you feel comfortable talking with this person. Every individual therapist is going to have his or her own personality, style, and treatment approach, and it's important that you find someone you feel right away that you can relate to.

If you care to, you can ask your therapist what therapeutic model he or she follows. The different models emphasize various aspects of psychological functioning, all of which may influence your behavior and mood. The basic models emphasize one or more of the following:

- Interpersonal (social)
- Psychodynamic

- ○ Cognitive (thinking)
- ○ Behavioral aspects of psychological functioning—all of which may affect how you feel or relate to others

But you don't have to really worry yourself about all that. Much more important is how you feel talking to this person. If there is a disconnect and you simply don't feel comfortable, make an appointment with another therapist. Keep going until you find someone you can really talk to. (And it's entirely possible that you'll find the right fit for you on the first try.)

Your first visit will be a consultation. Consultations are not free. Sometimes they are the same price as a regular session with the therapist and sometimes they are more expensive and, often, longer than the usual fifty-minute therapist's hour. Check your insurance: some companies will cover a higher fee for the consultation.

Use the consultation however you see fit. Feel free to ask the therapist about his or her training, background, experience, and style. Or use it as a first session. Either way, you should get a feel for the way the therapist conducts sessions.

HOW THERAPY WORKS

In the first few therapy sessions, some kind of determination will be made about your emotional state. If your symptoms are severe and even partially incapacitating, your need for medication will also be evaluated. If you are prescribed an antidepressant medication, it is imperative that you use it in conjunction with your therapy treatment and not instead of it. While the medication may help to balance the brain chemistry that affects mood and behavior, the therapy deals with underlying psychological issues and helps to identify and resolve conflicts that may go way back. Short-term therapy work will be helpful to a woman who just wants to deal with the immediate crisis.

Short-Term Therapy

In short-term work, the therapist provides encouragement and help in sorting out what steps, behaviorally and emotionally, you need to take to feel better. While short-term therapy may be all you need to get back on your feet, you may find in the process that there are significant unresolved conflicts (possibly going back to childhood) that make it impossible to move emotionally ahead from this crisis without first addressing them. And this may require longer-term work.

Long-Term Therapy

Long-term therapy explores your earlier history with relationships, family, friends, and other significant figures from the past, and helps you understand how and why these relationships and experiences are affecting the way you are currently reacting to your loss. For instance, one Almost Bride might have an especially difficult time recovering from her fiancé's having broken off the engagement. Through therapy, she realizes the connection between her feelings about the breakup and the feelings she experienced as a little kid when her father left her mother and didn't contact the family for years. Long-term therapy helps her see the connection from her adult point of view rather than from her helpless child's vantage point.

TAKING ANTIDEPRESSANTS

If you feel overwhelmed by symptoms of your depression, medication may make the roller coaster easier to bear. Talk to your doctor or a therapist to help you decide if medication is right for you.

How Antidepressants Work

Most cases of clinical depression occur in response to a significant loss or trauma, particularly to a person genetically or psychologically susceptible to depression. The medical community generally believes that depression is not caused by a single factor but is experienced in response to an interaction of genetic, biochemical, and psychological factors.

It is believed that antidepressant medication corrects a chemical imbalance or dysfunction in the brains of depressed people. Antidepressants raise the level of *neurotransmitters,* which are believed to be important in fighting depression. In the hypothalamus, the part of the brain responsible for human emotions, there are tiny gaps between the nerve cells. Neurotransmitters are chemical messengers that brain cells use to communicate with one another by carrying messages across these gaps to a receptor on the other side.

When a neurotransmitter connects with its corresponding receptor, the cell fires and sends on the message. Once the message is sent, the neurotransmitter is absorbed into the cell or burned up by enzymes. When levels of neurotransmitters are abnormally low, messages can't get across and communication in the brain slows down.

It is believed that depression will result if there aren't enough of the neurotransmitters operating or if they aren't fitting into their respective receptors. There are over a hundred different kinds of neurotransmitters. The ones most talked about in terms of their significance to depression are norepinephrine, serotonin, and dopamine.[9]

There's been a long-known correlation between depression and problems with hormone regulation. But there is no clear-cut explanation of what actually happens to produce depression. Whether depression is directly related to abnormal levels of neurotransmitters or whether these low levels indirectly affect other neurotransmitters, which in turn affect our emotional state, still remains a question.

Classes of Antidepressants

The major classes of antidepressants are *monoamine oxidase inhibitors* (MAOIs), *tricyclics,* and *serotonin inhibitors* (often referred to as SSRIs for selective serotonin reuptake inhibitors). These classes affect different neurotransmitter systems in different ways. The MAOIs and tricyclics have been used for a much longer time than the SSRIs (which first came on the market in the form of the well-known drug Prozac). The tricyclic antidepressants raise the level of several different neurotransmitters (norepinephrine, epinephrine, serotonin, and dopamine) by blocking their reabsorption. The MAOIs raise the neurotransmitter levels by destroying enzymes that burn up neurotransmitters. The SSRIs interfere with the reabsorption of the specific neurotransmitter serotonin.[10]

The SSRIs are prescribed most frequently nowadays because they seem to work at least as effectively as the older antidepressants and have much less significant, if any, side effects. The SSRIs that are commonly prescribed include Prozac (the generic drug name is fluoxetine, which has just recently become available in this form), Celexa (citalopram), Luvox (fluvoxamine), Zoloft (sertraline), and Paxil (paroxetine).

A newer strategy is to combine two medications for a more treatment-resistant depression. What is usually combined is one of the SSRIs with either a tricyclic or possibly a mood stabilizer (which helps level out the emotions of those who experience significant highs and lows). This is sometimes done to minimize side effects (since both medications are prescribed together at dosages lower than they would be alone), and it's been discovered that often each medication can boost the other. The process of finding the best medication, and sometimes a combination of medications, can take a number of trials of different antidepressants but is often worth the time and discomfort of mostly temporary side effects, like reduced libido, dizziness, and insomnia.

A PERSONAL CHOICE

Choosing to see a therapist is a personal choice. In my case, I wanted to see if there was a way to suffer less intensely and for a shorter period of time. I truly believe therapy helped me in both ways. Whatever you decide, don't refuse to consider therapy for fear that others will think you "crazy" or "unstable." A broken engagement is a traumatic event for most of us, and taking control of your mental health is just as important as watching over your physical health.

Chapter

10

New Beginnings

I think up until about two years after the breakup, I didn't really realize the enormity of what I had done. It was then that I realized that I had this pattern in my life, this weird fairy tale picture of what life and love were supposed to be. I thought it was supposed to be like it was in the movies: you meet, fall in love, get married, and live happily ever after. My ex-fiancé taught me that you can love someone, you can think that he is a great person, you can love spending time with him, and still not want to marry him. For me, that was an earth-shattering realization. I mean, I was raised my whole life to believe in this fairy tale, and to find out that it wasn't true was life-changing for me.

—DANA

For those of us with broken engagements, Happily Ever After has a whole new meaning.

MY STORY

In the days after Mark called an end to our half-baked fairy tale, I was set upon by friends. Debbie asked, "What do you need?" and I answered, "To walk." So she bundled her infant daughter into the car, drove into Manhattan, and we walked around the city for hours, with stops for a pedicure and lunch. Kim cooked me dinner, and when I said, "This hurts like hell, but it's absolutely the right thing," she grabbed a pen and paper and we wrote a long list of *why* it was the right thing, so I could remember the specifics when I faltered. Martin told me to call any time, so I woke him up at 2 A.M. and we talked in the dark till four.

All of this helped me immensely, but I still had to feel the pain. Home with my family, I cried. I cried while my mother held me, I cried myself to sleep, I burst into tears over lunch with my beloved cousins from Tel Aviv, who had planned to fly to America to attend my wedding and instead came in to make sure (like everyone else) that I ate.

One week later, I had a dream. Mark came back and stood at the edges of my garden, peering over shrubs and branches, his face obscured by leaves.

"I'm back!" he announced, as if I should be joyous.

"No," I told him, bodily defending the edges of my space, "you can't come in. That's it. It's over."

And when I woke up, I had more energy, I had my resolve. I still cried, but I didn't feel like it would never stop. I went back to Washington, and to work. When Mark's sister-in-law called a few days later and asked if she could help in any way, I thanked her and told her firmly that it was over. I asked her to understand that I couldn't see her and my amazing "nieces" again and asked her to please take care of him, and I waited till the phone was safely in its cradle and I was out on the street before I cried. A small difference maybe, but if she had called any earlier, I couldn't have choked out the words.

A month later, I was signing the lease on a new apartment, drinking less, and sleeping better. I still felt tangibly sad and lost almost all the time, but I was on my knees instead of flat on my ass.

Six months later, I had begun to date regularly, had gained back the weight I had lost, and never cried. My friend Susie called to check in on me from Atlanta and delighted at "the smile" in my voice. I no longer thought of Mark every day—though I still dreamed about his dog, whom I miss to this day. (In fact, I never dreamed about Mark again after he almost invaded my garden.) More and more, I felt I was "over" Mark. But I wasn't yet over the feeling that I had stepped out of the path of a speeding train. I was thankful every single day that I hadn't married him.

One year later, I am a new woman. Happier than I have ever been, I'm both freer and more intense. I know myself better, and I like what I see. My broken engagement—and the suffering I went through—changed my life for the better. I no longer think I've sidestepped disaster; I simply don't think about it. I'm back!

I'M OK, YOU'RE OK

"Am I normal?"

As I rode my personal roller coaster, I wondered that often.

You can't help but wonder, too, when *you* called it off and you can't eat. Or he called it off and you've lost interest in your favorite things, and since *when* are you that pathetic? Or it's mutual and for the best and you're relieved and crying all the time anyway.

If you are feeling awful, I promise you: you're normal.

But you're also normal if you're *not* feeling awful. Some Almost Brides report feeling wonderfully relieved from the moment they called it off. What all Almost Brides come to realize is that with time comes the ability to move on, and though the tunnel through is often slick, smelly, and close, there *is* light on the other side.

I asked Almost Brides, how would you describe yourself and your life in the week after calling it off?

I was really feeling strong and confident in the decision. I told everyone and had a lot of energy to do activities for myself and go out with others. I don't remember crying. —LILLY

I was miserable. Couldn't eat, sleep, or leave the house. —GRETCHEN

I was relatively normal. Cried every now and then and thought about John a lot, but I remained convinced that I had done the right thing. I spent a lot of time with my family and talking with my friends. Luckily, I was very busy at work, so I didn't have a lot of time to dwell on things during the day. —MATTIE

I was upset. I felt very guilty. —AMY

I was a mess. I wasn't eating or exercising. I walked around like a zombie. I felt drained of all my energy and I didn't feel like doing anything. I went to work but I was basically just a waste of space. I felt like that scene in *Ally McBeal* when she gets shot repeatedly with arrows. That was the picture of how I felt at the time. Even the sound effects seemed accurate! —SOPHIE

I was suffering mostly while we were together. I really felt liberated after calling the wedding off. I was trying to avoid him the week after calling it off. I was doing well and spending time with friends. —BETSY

I wasn't eating, I wasn't sleeping, but I still had to go to work. I literally was living on coffee and nicotine. I lost so much weight and I cried all the time. I felt like a failure and I had no self-respect. Somehow, I felt like I was still the bad guy.   —PELLA

A mess. I could not make a decision if I had to. I slept a lot and cried rivers.   —ANDREA

I immediately left the state for a planned trip to visit my best friend. I was in shock but felt immense relief.   —DEE DEE

I was in a daze. Trying to figure out when I could go back to the apartment and get more of my stuff without running into him. Also, customers at work keep asking me how the wedding planning was going, and it was hard not to just start crying.   —KELLY

I felt free the week after we broke up. Even though he tried to harass me by having others call me and e-mail me, I had never felt better.

—JOAN

A complete mess.   —FIONA

Very pissed off and very upset that I had been taken. I was also frightfully embarrassed to tell people that the engagement had been called off.

—HILARY

I was in disbelief that I had had the courage to do it.   —MARCI

I was not living. I was a walking zombie, not eating, showering, sleeping, or working.   —STACEY

A little unnerved at not having anyone. It was hard to get used to being alone, especially in a brand-new town where I only knew my roommate (and I had just met her the first day of school!).   —ROBIN

I saw many friends and family and kept myself busy. Being alone was not easy and I tried to avoid it as much as possible.   —LAURA

I spent a lot of time decorating my new bedroom. I was upset; I believed I didn't fit in anywhere. I was borrowing my sisters' clothing, as my clothes were at my old home. I felt like I was a mess, with no strength to carry on. I felt relieved and not scared, but so confused.   —SANDY

Still on autopilot. I mean, this was supposed to be the last seven days before my wedding! Still trying to cancel stuff and make immediate decisions required to move on.   —JESSICA

I asked Almost Brides, how would you describe yourself and your life in the month after calling it off?

After two weeks, I started feeling sadder and more lost. I realized my whole life plan was altered, and it's a lot to deal with.   —LILLY

Same as the first week. Felt like I had failed miserably.   —GRETCHEN

Things got easier, I cried less. Still thought about him a lot—mainly because I still ran into him on occasion or talked to his sister. I packed up all of the stuff [related to him] and put it away, which made things a lot easier. My life basically got back to normal. I did a lot of thinking about where I wanted to go from here, what I wanted to do with my life. I still don't know, but I have some ideas.   —MATTIE

Recovering quite nicely. Still felt guilty, probably mainly because I was doing so well so quickly.   —AMY

Total turnaround! That was just after 9/11 and—not to minimize it—that was a distraction [from my own problems]. My life was brand new and I was excited.   —SOPHIE

There was a noticeable improvement in my personality and my self-confidence.

—BETSY

Same, except I was starting to eat a bit better. And at that point, I started to get high every day to cope.

—PELLA

More aggressive on things I wanted. Taking care of myself and healing broken friendships.

—ANDREA

He wanted to talk and reconcile, but I was strong and refused to get back together. I think my strength surprised me, but I kept wondering, "Is this really it? I really left him?"

—DEE DEE

I was a little better. Was laughing with my new roomies and going out some. Still slept a lot.

—KELLY

I fell in love hard with a man who treated me wonderfully, a complete 180 from my ex.

—JOAN

A complete mess.

—FIONA

I began to remember the good parts of our relationship and wanted my best friend back.

—HILARY

I have become the person I used to be again. I am happy, strong-minded, and willing to be a little flirtatious at times. I am happier now than I have been in years.

—MARCI

Still very depressed, finally working, and pretending to be going on with my life.

—STACEY

Still alone but happy and confident in my choice to call it off. I felt empowered and free. I'd dated a few other guys, but no one special.

—ROBIN

I began feeling better, but then we started talking again about getting back together. Big mistake. —LAURA

He had started to stalk me and the guilt was nearly unbearable. I didn't want to be close to anyone. —SANDY

Free! Making decisions that affected me only. Trying to see which way to go with life. Still grappling with the fact that I had actually called it off.

—JESSICA

I asked Almost Brides, how would you describe yourself and your life in the six months after calling it off?

I wanted to take it all back and try again. —GRETCHEN

In a new, fulfilling relationship with my friend Tom, not believing how wonderful and different it was to be in a mutually caring, loving relationship with someone who shared his feelings with me on a regular basis. Still enjoying college. I was feeling very good about myself and my place in the world. —AMY

He is a distant memory. Luckily, he doesn't live around here, so I don't have to worry about bumping into him. That's a nice luxury. I'm back in college and live my life on my own terms. —SOPHIE

In the six months after we broke up, a very close friend of mine, Joe, died in an accident. My ex-fiancé told me—a week after the accident, on the day of the funeral—that I needed to talk to him, and I had had a week to get over Joe's death. That reassured me that I had made the right decision.

—BETSY

I met my current fiancé six months after calling it off. We were only friends for years, but I had found a new circle of friends I adored, and it was at that time that I became determined to stop dwelling in the past and move on with my life. To me, that meant to start dating, but that wasn't really the best thing for me either.   —PELLA

Happy and content with life itself. Was meeting my future fiancé at a Halloween party.   —ANDREA

I traveled, got reacquainted with some old friends, and changed positions at my company.   —DEE DEE

I had moved to yet another place [and] was having occasional dates but no sex. Still missed his kids, but overall was realizing how I really *was* better off.   —KELLY

I had broken up the next relationship, too (it was doomed to fail), and was working on getting myself back in line with who I am and what I wanted for myself.   —JOAN

It was dawning on me that if I didn't start to live again, I would never be over it.   —FIONA

By the six-month point of calling off my engagement . . . [my new boyfriend] Larry and I were already talking about moving in together.
                                        —HILARY

Still deeply in love with him, starting to date somewhat, but would go back to him in a heartbeat; still in contact with him.   —STACEY

I had just begun dating my husband! I was giddy with happiness and doing great in all my coursework at school. I had a lot of friends and felt really great about my life.   —ROBIN

[Our contact] finally ended about five months later and that was when I truly felt relieved. I began making plans for what I wanted out of life. The biggest was to get out of that city!   —LAURA

I had a lot of problems with friends who wanted to stand by both him and me. I didn't want any ties to him, so I lost a lot of friends, but I gained a lot of respect for myself. I am really proud of what I've achieved.

—SANDY

In a truly good place. Positively looking forward to the experiences that life will bring. Open to the experiences. —JESSICA

I asked Almost Brides, how would you describe yourself and your life in the year after calling it off?

I was miserable again. We were back together and he was worse than before. —GRETCHEN

Living with Tom, talking very seriously of marriage. Very, very happy; happier than I had ever been in my life. I felt very complete. Still going to college and loving it. Bought a house with Tom . . . feeling so good, it was kind of scary. —AMY

In the year after, I had graduated from grad school, been involved in another serious relationship, called it off, and was surviving on my own at a fabulous job with fabulous friends. I was working constantly and enjoying every minute of it! —BETSY

I was partying a lot and making bad decisions in terms of the men I was dating. There were probably two guys I dated in that year that I slept with and really shouldn't have, but I needed to feel validated and made bad choices for myself. —PELLA

Happy, content, strong, and determined not to make the same mistakes. Was dating future fiancé. —ANDREA

I had bought a house, started dating again (although no one seriously), and was very happy and content. —DEE DEE

I realized what a complete idiot I was for staying with him for so long! But it was hard to get back into another relationship, because I simply didn't trust anyone. I didn't trust *myself* to accurately gauge how well a relationship was going, because my judgment had obviously been *so* wrong with him.

—KELLY

I met my current fiancé and had begun to make a life with him.

—JOAN

I slowly got back on track. I met up with old friends who took me under their wing. Started going out and enjoying myself again. —FIONA

Meeting Larry made me realize how much I would have been settling for with Peter. True, Peter and I had a very personal connection, but there were too many differences between our expectations out of life. Larry and I are absolutely a match made in heaven, and I have never doubted that.

—HILARY

Not in love with him but still have strong feelings for him. Almost enjoying life at times. Think about him at least once a day. —STACEY

Still dating my husband; we might have broken up once by then, though. This would be the drunken party stage of my life—full of clubs and friends and lots of drinking. Also my first year with my own apartment. Lots of freedom. Grades? Well, they slipped a little! —ROBIN

I met a wonderful guy who I never thought would like me. Nothing came of it, but it made me see that there are men out there who are better suited for me. I was so much happier. —LAURA

I've got a new job, new car, new house, am about to move to a new city, and I'm planning a wedding with a wonderful fiancé who I feel 100 percent confident about. I am learning that my plans with my ex weren't just his problems (although they mostly were), and am trying to create a harmonic relationship with my partner. It has only been eleven months since I left my ex, and my life is wonderful! I've lost a lot of friends, but I am much closer to my family, and, of course, Bob, my soul mate. —SANDY

In love! I met a wonderful man who opened the door to a better relationship. —JESSICA

I asked Almost Brides, how would you describe yourself and your life now?

I don't know what I ever saw in him. I am strong, happy, and sure of myself, and I have learned what real love, true friendship, and family is all about. I am where I wanted to be. —GRETCHEN

Tom and I are engaged. We are extremely happy; however, we both know that our relationship takes constant work—that communication is the biggest part of a successful relationship, and that in order to make it, we are going to have to work on our relationship continuously. I am still in school. I know that I got to this place, to be able to be this healthy and happy, because of my relationship with my ex. I would never appreciate the sharing nor understand the importance of communication that's in my life now—not only with Tom, but with everyone around me. —AMY

My firm has gone under and I've found a new job that I love. I truly believe that things happen for a reason. I'm talking to him, but I don't need him and he has no control over me. I'm seeing some other people, just trying to figure things out. —BETSY

I ended very long-standing relationships—friends from grade school and on, but those were friends who supported my drug habit, and I needed to get away from that. I'm now clean and have been for a few years. I developed a relationship with a wonderful man who was my best friend for four years. We started dating on a bet just over a year ago, and this December, we'll be married. I am truly marrying my best friend. It took a long time for us to get to this point, but after the way my last relationship shattered me, I needed to make sure I was doing everything right this time.

—PELLA

I am more centered, controlled, and happy about everything. I am engaged to be married to the man of my dreams. He has given me reason to trust and love again. —ANDREA

A happy newlywed of eight months. I have a good job; we plan to have kids soon. We travel, we share common interests, and we are enjoying building our life together. —DEE DEE

Now I am truly a happy person! I still have scars from the previous engagement, but we all have our scars. —KELLY

My life is wonderful. I work full-time, I go to school part-time, and I have gone back to having the few close friends [who] make me happiest. I have a wonderful man who loves me dearly and I feel the same back. We are planning a wedding for seven months from now and are having a blast planning our future together. He accepts me for who I am and who I want to be. I think of myself as very lucky. —JOAN

My personality hasn't changed much: I am still depressed on the inside and confident on the outside. I now take pride in my appearance. Life has changed enormously. I married a wonderful man who I love very much, I have a good job, I own my own home, and I basically feel that I am back on track, doing the things that made me happy. —FIONA

Content. I don't like my job, but I plan on going back to grad school next year. My husband and I are happy. A few minor bumps in the road (we've been married three months), but we are working through them. We just bought our first house and everything is going pretty well. —ROBIN

[My fiancé and I broke up completely] about four years ago. I now live in Washington and love it! I love my life and no longer worry about meeting the right person, and have no regrets about calling that off. I have a confidence that I would have never had if I had not gone through that experience. —LAURA

I am truly happy. I won't say that I am fulfilled, because that would make it seem like there wasn't much more for me to do with life. And I think I have a whole lot left to do, and give to others, before my life ends.

—JESSICA

BROKEN ENGAGEMENTS HELP
FUTURE RELATIONSHIPS

A broken engagement is the gift that keeps on giving. You can be held back by it, or you can fly forward. Almost Bride Stacey is still learning to be vulnerable again:

I'm very leery. I am so afraid that someone is going to say he loves me and not mean it, and I will get hurt all over again. So I tend to keep men at a distance.

But it doesn't have to be that way. In addition to giving you an air of mystery forever after, the experience can keep you honest about your needs *and* help you get those needs met.

I asked Almost Brides, how, if at all, did going through a broken engagement help your present relationship?

The learning process that ensued after calling it off was invaluable to my present relationship. Having my old relationship end gave me an opportunity to reevaluate my priorities and establish a list of "deal breakers" that I would never allow into a relationship ever again. My deal breakers list

included, among other things, that I would never allow myself to become seriously involved with someone who had drastically different familial values from mine and that I would never become seriously involved with someone who considered his career top priority, above me. Beyond developing a better perspective on relationships, calling it off allowed me to see that I could make it independent of my ex. It proved to me that I was stronger and more capable than I thought.
—CAROLYN

I now know what to look out for when I get in relationships. My relationships are much healthier now.
—BETSY

I am casually seeing someone. [Going through a broken engagement] has made me more aware of my partner, and I know that if I see something I don't like, I will not ignore it like I used to.
—MARCI

It made me more aware of what really makes a man a "good" man. It taught me a lot about myself—both good and bad, and I think I could bring that into [my current] relationship.
—WINNIE

I knew what to look for in a man, really. I knew there wasn't a perfect man, but I knew what I didn't want. I could see it sooner. I was older, a little jaded, and I was going slowly into that big thing called the real world. Anyway, my husband is the exact opposite of that loser, so I'm happy.
—SAMANTHA

It helped me understand how important our families are to the relationship. It also made me very nervous about anything that appeared to be smothering or controlling. I think it is partly thanks to that that we have a fairly balanced relationship. If anything, I am more standoffish than my husband—a bit of role reversal that works quite well for us.
—ABBY

I know how I want to be treated and I treat my husband the same way.
—ANSEL

I learned to appreciate how my fiancé treats me and how he's honest with me, and we're willing to work through anything. We had to go to counseling, but it has made us stronger. —AVERY

I'm not in a relationship, but it has still helped me. I know that I will not settle for just anyone. I've learned to listen to the people around me when they say something about my relationship. I learned that I may be too close to the situation to see it for what it really is. It seemed like I was always defending him to people, and it turns out the people I thought were being so hurtful to me were seeing things for what they really were. That is something I chose not to do at the time. —SOPHIE

It helped tremendously. It probably helped bring my fiancé and I together. It helped me to understand what "good" love is and what "bad" love is.

—MELISSA

It helped immensely. I was able to accept my responsibility for my part in the relationship and see where I went wrong. I make sure I do not make the same mistakes now. I came out of that relationship so much stronger and independent than I ever was. —ERIN

There was never a moment, as difficult as it would have been, that I would have hesitated to leave [my current relationship] if it looked as though we were not meant to be together—if our goals were different, or our values, or our hopes for the future.

As painful as it would have been, I knew that I would survive it and go on to find [the man] I was supposed to be with. It was the time with [my ex] that provided me that strength. And in that strength I developed confidence, and in that confidence I developed trust, and in that trust I developed love.

Two years after meeting, Andy and I were married, and I have never been happier. —BECKA

I believe that everything we experience in life contributes to our character, beliefs, and personality—everything we are. And the woman I am, the
woman Greg loves, would be a different woman if I hadn't gone through
that. He says the thing he admires most about me is my strength, and
[leaving] that relationship is where it came from.   —PELLA

ON FROM HERE

I know it's scary to contemplate being vulnerable again, but
the Almost Brides prove that the best is really yet to be. Just
remember:

- Choose a partner who meets your needs, not a partner you like *despite* his inability to meet them.
- Approach relationships without the fantasy that you
  can change your partner.
- Voice your needs.
- Assert yourself if you want to get out of the
  relationship.

Having gone through a broken engagement, you now
know what you need, and you're in a position to get it—from
relationships and from yourself.

MY STORY
❀

Sometimes I can't believe a full year has gone by. Most of
the time, though, I feel like it's been years since I was
planning that wedding. It's not just the difference in how

good I feel physically without the corroding stress, it's the emotional distance and the progress on myself that makes my engagement seem like it was a lifetime ago.

No, I haven't fallen in love again. I did date someone for six months, but for many reasons we weren't meant to go the distance. When we broke up, I was sorely tempted to buy him flowers. I'm sure he wouldn't have understood why, and I didn't want to make him uncomfortable, so I didn't.

But it's like this: after my broken engagement, I felt like nothing made sense anymore. Not me, not the world. All those clichés felt so true: the sky fell in. I dodged a bullet. I was kicked in the gut.

Caring deeply for someone again was truly like a rebirth.

I look forward to doing it again.

Epilogue

❀ ❀ ❀

Some women get over their broken engagements by throwing themselves into work or the next relationship or partying. I got over mine by writing this book.

When I posted on the chat boards of The Knot for the umpteenth time that I had cold feet, and this time my fiancé had started to get chilly, too, one woman's response stood out among the dozens of virtual "hang in there!"s and hugs.

"Look at it this way," she wrote. "One way or the other, in one year, you will be happy again." She urged me to look ahead from this trying time to my happy future.

I read that post and instantly thought: the only way I'll be happy a year from now is if I call off this wedding.

I knew that for a fact, and yet I still hung tight.

Regardless of who calls it off, there is so much more to a broken engagement than a broken heart. There's a kernel of failure that sticks in our ribs. There's a fear we've done the wrong thing and ruined the rest of our lives. There's a tidal wave of being overwhelmed at the party-planning t's we have to uncross and the i's that will have to be undotted. A broken engagement is a very public breakup, and since we're not earning the salary of Julia Roberts, that's not something we should have to endure.

I knew what I wanted and I couldn't do it. This book is about figuring out your own heart and doing what *you* need to do. That might be getting your butt into premarital counseling. It may mean breaking your engagement. And it may be forgiving your fiancé for calling off your wedding, and moving on.

Writing *There Goes the Bride* helped me through. I hope reading it did the same for you.

Check out www.theregoesthebride.com to chat with other Almost Brides and get updates, and please stay in touch. I and sixty-two Almost Brides send a hug.

And remember: your Big Day isn't just your wedding day—it's every day.

Best,
Rachel Safier

Resources

Premarital Counseling
Find Help Fast
Breakup Movies
Songs to Sing at the Top of Your Lungs
Sayings to Get You Through the Day
The Almost Brides
The Almost Brides' Survey

Premarital Counseling

❀ ❀ ❀

There are many outlets for the cold-footed to pursue before calling it quits. Some of the most popular are listed here. For more on the concept of premarital counseling, see Chapter Two.

FOCCUS

According to familyministries.org, FOCCUS (Facilitating Open Couple Communication, Understanding and Study) is

an internationally used instrument for marriage preparation. It is self-diagnostic and designed to help couples learn more about themselves and their unique relationship. It provides individualized couple feedback on where each partner stands in regard to topic areas important to marriage. FOCCUS was developed to reflect the values and ideals of marriage as sacred. It is recommended as an early step in marriage preparation.

FOCCUS is faith-based, with questions on Christian belief and interfaith differences.

For more information: see Chapter Two for sample questions from FOCCUS. Contact your clergy member to be set up with a mentor couple, who will guide you through the process.

PREPARE

Offered by Life Innovations, Inc., PREPARE "is not a 'test' per se," says Luke Knutson, research associate at Life Innovations. "It's an inventory to give couples an idea of the strengths and growth areas in their relationship." Forty-five thousand trained counselors have administered the inventory to more than one million couples since 1980. Each inventory has 165 items and thirty background questions. PREPARE scores the answers, returning a computer report to a counselor to discuss with the couple. PREPARE is a secular inventory.

The test costs $30 to score, per couple. Since the answers are returned to a counselor, the cost is variable, depending on whether you see a member of the clergy or a therapist. Most couples meet with their counselor three to six times after taking the test.

For more information: go to Life Innovation's Web site, at www.lifeinnovations.com. There, you'll find a list of trained counselors in your area.

PRE-CANA

Couples choosing to marry in the Catholic Church are required to engage in counseling with their clergyman. Sample issues raised in pre-Cana are offered in Chapter Two.

For more information: contact your clergy member.

CATHOLIC ENGAGED ENCOUNTER

With the tag line "A Wedding Is a Day, a Marriage Is a Lifetime," Catholic Engaged Encounter offers participants a weekend of reflection to "deepen your relationship with each other and with God." Engaged Encounter is led by Church volunteers. Weekends last from Friday night to Sunday afternoon and cost an average of $157 per engaged couple. Five percent of couples receive financial aid.

Each group of couples is led by a senior couple (married for more than ten years), a junior couple, and a priest. Topics covered include communications, prayer, forgiveness, and natural family planning. The Center for the Applied Research in the Apostate (CARA) at Georgetown University provides these statistics on those attending:

- Average Age: 27
- Average number of months in relationship: 36
- Percentage living with fiancé: 44
- Percentage who attend Mass at least once a week: 47

Couples are encouraged to attend six months before their wedding; priests may require couples they will be marrying to attend.

For more information: contact your priest or your local diocese, or visit www.engagedencounter.org. Information on engaged encounters for Christian non-Catholics can be found on the Engaged Encounter Web site. Both the 1997 *Catholic Engaged Encounter Renewal* and the 1998 *Catholic Engaged Encounter Follow-Up Participant Study* may be ordered from CARA. Contact CARA in Washington, D.C., by phone at 202-687-8080 or fax 202-687-8083.

MARRIAGE COUNSELING

If you'd prefer to meet with a counselor and not follow a set counseling regime or inventory, contact the American Psychiatric Association, the American Psychological Association, or National Association of Social Workers to find a therapist trained in premarital counseling.

For more information: contact information for these associations is listed in the next Resource, Find Help Fast.

Find Help
Fast

❀ ❀ ❀

Don't be afraid to ask for more help.

FIND A THERAPIST NEAR YOU

For the differences between these types of therapists, see
Chapter Nine.

To find a psychiatrist:
Contact the American Psychiatric Association
888-357-7924
http://www.psych.org/public_info/choose_a_psy.cfm
(www.psych.org for the Association's homepage)

To find a psychologist:
Contact the American Psychological Association
800-964-2000
http://helping.apa.org/find.html
(www.apa.org for the Association's homepage)

To find a social worker:
Contact the National Association of Social Workers
202-408-8600 (in Washington, D.C.)
http://www.socialworkers.org/register/default.asp
(www.naswdc.org for the association's homepage)

IF YOU'RE AFRAID YOU'LL HURT YOURSELF

Contact the National Suicide Hotline
800-SUICIDE

IF YOUR PARTNER/EX IS HURTING YOU
OR YOU FEAR HE MAY

Contact the National Coalition Against Domestic Violence
Hotline
800-799-7233 (**for immediate assistance, dial 911**)
http://www.ncadv.org

IF YOU SUSPECT YOU HAVE A DRINKING PROBLEM

Contact Alcoholics Anonymous
Look in the phone book for local meetings or call AA world
headquarters in New York at 212-870-3400
http://www.alcoholics-anonymous.org

IF YOU SUSPECT YOUR PARTNER/EX
HAS A DRINKING PROBLEM

Contact Al-Anon
Call 888-4AL-ANON for meetings in the United States and
    Canada
http://www.al-anon.alateen.org

Breakup Movies

Raid the local Blockbuster and curl up on the couch with these suggestions from women who know. The movies are rated CA for cackling or CR for crying.

The First Wives Club (CA)

Chicken Run (CA)

Romy and Michelle's High School Reunion (CA)

When Harry Met Sally (CR)

Waiting to Exhale (CA and CR)

Mr. Wonderful (CR)

Thelma and Louise (CA)

How Stella Got Her Groove Back (CA)

American Pie (CA)

Swingers (CA)

Bridget Jones's Diary (CA)

Grease (CA)

Steel Magnolias (CR)

Better Off Dead (CA)

10 Things I Hate About You (CA)

Mystic Pizza (CA and CR)

Terms of Endearment (CR)

Shag (CA)

When a Man Loves a Woman (CR)

Hush (Neither a barrel of monkeys nor a tearjerker, this one is guaranteed to make you exclaim, "Thank *God* I didn't marry into that family!")

Songs to Sing at the Top of Your Lungs

❋ ❋ ❋

These songs fulfill Almost Bride Teri's criteria for must-sing breakup songs: they're "cheesy songs that you can belt out in the car . . . [and] songs my ex would have *refused* to listen to."

Gloria Gaynor, "I Will Survive"

JoDee Messina, "Bye Bye"

Jennifer Lopez, "I'm Gonna Be Alright"

Dixie Chicks, "Let Him Fly"

Alanis Morissette, "Narcissus"

Pink, "There You Go"

Jackson Browne, "I'm Alive"

Celine Dion, "That's the Way It Is"

Pat Benatar, "All Fired Up"

Destiny's Child, "Survivor"

Chely Wright, "Shut Up and Drive"

Ace of Base, "It's a Beautiful Life"

ABBA, "So Long"

Travis Tritt, "It's a Great Day to Be Alive"

Sayings to Get You Through the Day

❀ ❀ ❀

(With thanks to BrainyQuotes.com, the Almost Brides, and my friends the Sunnies)

Never be bullied into silence. Never allow yourself to be made a victim. Accept no one's definition of your life; define yourself.

—HARVEY FIERSTEIN

Finish each day and be done with it. You have done what you could; some blunders and absurdities have crept in; forget them as soon as you can. Tomorrow is a new day; you shall begin it serenely and with too high a spirit to be encumbered with your old nonsense.

—RALPH WALDO EMERSON

You cannot prevent the birds of sorrow from flying over your head, but you don't have to let them make nests in your hair.

—CHINESE PROVERB

Peace. It does not mean to be in a place where there is no noise, trouble or hard work. It means to be in the midst of all those things and still be calm in your heart.

—UNKNOWN

Never compromise yourself. You're all you've got.

—JANIS JOPLIN

When someone shows you who he is, believe him.

—MAYA ANGELOU

For every minute you remain angry, you give up sixty seconds of peace of mind.

—RALPH WALDO EMERSON

Better to call it off than wind up like Elizabeth Taylor.

—ALMOST BRIDE KATE'S BEST FRIEND

The world owes you nothing. It was here first.

—MARK TWAIN

Experience is not what happens to you; it is what you do with what happens to you.

—ALDOUS HUXLEY

Always write angry letters to your enemies. Never mail them.

—JAMES FALLOWS

Thank you, God, for what I have. And thank you for what I don't.

—MY NIGHTLY PRAYER

The best revenge is going on to live a wonderful life.

—DAVID SCHWARTZ

When life gives you lemons, stuff 'em in your bra.

—UNKNOWN

The Almost Brides

❀ ❀ ❀

Name, year of birth, age at broken engagement, state (or country, if not the USA) of residence:

Abby, 1971, 18, Connecticut
Amy, 1969, 29, Ohio
Andrea, 1973, 25, Missouri
Ansel, 1979, 21, Georgia
Avery, 1973, 23, Ohio
Becka, 1973, 26, Washington
Betsy, 1979, 21, Virginia
Bonnie, 1978, 23, South Carolina
Carol, 1975, 23, California
Carolyn, 1975, 25, Florida

Christine, 1973, 29, Missouri
Claudia, 1969, 31, Canada
Dana, 1976, 19, Illinois
Danielle, 1978, 17, South Dakota
Dawn, 1968, 31, New Jersey
Debbie, 1977, 23, New Jersey
Dee Dee, 1964, 29, Oregon
Diana, 1972, 29, Ohio
Donna, 1977, 22, Pennsylvania
Elly, 1968, 22, New York
Elizabeth, 1975, 20 and 23, New York
Erin, 1975, 24, Ohio
Fiona, 1975, 23, England
Gretchen, 1970, 19, Canada
Hannah, 1970, 23, Maryland
Heather, 1979, 23, Texas
Hilary, 1974, 25, Missouri
Jane, 1980, 20, District of Columbia
Jennifer, 1966, 31, Wisconsin
Jessica, 1967, 28, Virginia
Jill, 1971, 30, Alabama
Joan, 1977, 20, Michigan
Jodi, 1980, 19, Maryland
Kate, 1972, 25, New York
Kim, 1973, 26, New York
Karen, 1966, 29, Washington State
Kelly, 1966, 28, Tennessee
Laura, 1965, 31, Virginia
Lilly, 1973, 28, Massachusetts
Lisa, 1980, 22, Missouri

Lucy, 1976, 23, Florida
Lynn, 1977, 22, New York
Marci, 1979, 22, California
Martha, 1969, 33, Missouri
Mattie, 1978, 23, Arkansas
Melissa, 1977, 22, Michigan
Naomi, 1945, 20, New York
Natalie, 1965, 26 and 32, Maryland
Pella, 1974, 22, Illinois
Robin, 1978, 19, Michigan
Roxy, 1955, 22, 24, 28, and 35, District of Columbia
Samantha, 1975, 22, Maryland
Sandy, 1976, 24, Australia
Sophie, 1973, 28, Michigan
Susan, 1974, 23, New Jersey
Stacey, 1980, 21, Massachusetts
Tamara, 1970, 30, District of Columbia
Teri, 1975, 24, North Carolina
Tracy, 1976, 24, Ohio
Valerie, 1976, 25, New York
Winnie, 1970, 23, Georgia
Zoë, 1973, 26, Connecticut

The Almost Brides' Survey

❊ ❊ ❊

I distributed this survey to the Almost Brides and got back thoughtful, thorough answers about their lives before, during, and after their engagements. Recently, a woman e-mailed me and asked if she could take a look at the survey. She was engaged and unhappy, and a friend, an Almost Bride who participated in the making of this book, suggested she take the survey to help her sort through her feelings.

I've included the survey here in the hope it can do the same for you, whether you're suffering from cold feet or have gone through a broken engagement (regardless of whether you called it off or your fiancé did).

All the Almost Brides who took part thanked me for the cathartic experience of taking this survey. Interestingly, many of the women whose fiancés had called off their weddings found that they, too, had seen the end of the relationship coming. But it was only after they organized their thoughts—thanks to the survey—that they realized it.

CALLING IT OFF

I. Background
1. *Describe yourself.*
2. *Describe your ideas of marriage before you met your ex. Have those ideas changed? How?*

II. Life before calling it off
1. *Describe your life before you met your ex.*
2. *Describe yourself before you met your ex.*
3. *How did your life change, if at all, when you met (became involved with) him?*
4. *How did you change, if at all, when you met him?*
5. *If you changed, why did you change?*
6. *Describe meeting him.*
7. *Why did you want to date him?*
8. *Why did you want to marry him?*
9. *Who brought up the idea of getting married first? How? How did the other party react?*
10. *How long did you date (give your ages as well) before discussing marriage?*
11. *How long did you date before getting lengaged?*
12. *Who asked whom?*

13. *Describe the proposal. What were the circumstances and what did the asker say?*
14. *What did the respondent say?*
15. *If you were the respondent, do you remember exactly how you felt when you were asked?*
16. *If you asked, do you remember exactly how you felt when you asked?*
17. *What did you do after the formal proposal?*
18. *Who did you tell first?*
19. *Who was the hardest to tell?*

III. Life with ex
1. *Describe your feelings for your ex when you were in love.*
2. *Did you live with your ex at any point?*
3. *Did this affect your relationship in any way?*
4. *What were your points of conflict before being engaged?*
5. *What were your points of conflict after getting engaged?*
6. *What were your favorite things about your ex?*
7. *What were your least favorite things about your ex?*
8. *Looking back, were there signs you chose to ignore? If so, what were they?*

IV. Wedding planning
1. *How long were you engaged before you called it off?*
2. *How much wedding planning did you do?*
3. *Describe the planning.*

4. *Which of these apply to you?*
   (a) I have always dreamed of my wedding
   (b) I never wanted to marry
   (c) I thought I'd marry, but I never thought about the details
   (d) I found planning the wedding stressful
   (e) I found planning the wedding fun
   (f) We weren't together long enough to begin planning
   (g) My parents made planning stressful
   (h) His parents made planning stressful
   (i) We made a wedding planning budget
   (j) We didn't make a wedding planning budget
   (k) We kept to our budget
   (l) We exceeded our budget

5. *Describe the religiosity of the wedding you were planning. Were you in agreement with each other on the level and type of religiosity? Were you in agreement with your families?*

6. *Describe the size of the wedding you were planning. Were you in agreement with each other? With your families?*

7. *Complete this sentence: the best part of planning was* _____

8. *Complete this sentence: the worst part of planning was* _____

V. Life planning

   1. *How much did you discuss the following topics?*

      (a) Money
      (b) Family (your original family and the one you would build together)
      (c) Work or school
      (d) Leisure activities
      (e) Friends
      (f) Future

  2. *How much did you agree on the following topics?*
      (a) Money
      (b) Family (your original family and the one you would build together)
      (c) Work or school
      (d) Leisure activities
      (e) Friends
      (f) Future

  3. *Expand on any conflict.*

VI. Calling it off

  1. *Explain why the wedding was called off.*
  2. *Who called it off?*
  3. *Explain the calling off in detail.*
  4. *How did you go about undoing the union—the wedding, the household, the relationship (whatever applies)?*
  5. *Could your relationship have been saved?*
  6. *Did you want it to be saved? If so, for how long after calling it off did you want it to be fixed?*
  7. *Was there any period of reconciliation? If so, how long did it last? Was going back for more the right choice for you? Why or why not?*

VII. After him
1. *For how long did you suffer?*
2. *How did your suffering manifest itself? How were your eating, sleeping, working, and exercising affected, if at all?*
3. *Who, if anyone, helped ease the suffering? How? For all of the following, give as many anecdotes as you wish.*
4. *What words of others gave you comfort?*
5. *What words of others gave you strength?*
6. *What acts of others gave you comfort?*
7. *What acts of yourself gave you comfort?*
8. *What acts of yourself gave you strength?*
9. *Can you recommend any comfort foods? Any comfort food recipes?*
10. *What books or movies, if any, gave you comfort or strength?*
11. *What words of others did not give you comfort or strength?*
12. *What acts of others did not give you comfort or strength?*
13. *What acts of yourself did not give you comfort or strength?*
14. *A woman who has just called off her wedding is standing here, in front of you. What do you tell her?*

VIII. Moving on
1. *Describe yourself and your life in the week after calling it off.*
2. *Describe yourself and your life in the month after calling it off.*

3. *Describe yourself and your life in the six months after calling it off.*

4. *Describe yourself and your life in the year after calling it off.*

5. *Describe yourself and your life now.*

6. *Fill in the blank: if you could have known _____ then, you wouldn't have believed it.*

7. *True or false? What doesn't kill you makes you stronger. (Why do you think this is so, or not?)*

8. *True or false? Everything happens for a reason. (Why do you think this is so, or not?)*

IX. Relationships after him

1. *Are you dating, in a relationship, engaged, or married now?*

2. *How, if at all, did going through what you went through help your present relationship, if you have one?*

3. *Describe your present relationship, if you have one.*

4. *How long did you wait before delving into the dating world again? Why?*

X. What else?

1. *What would a book of this type have needed to help you when you were going through calling it off?*

2. *What else would you like to tell me?*

Bonus question (suggested by a contributor): Did you *know* before you knew? Explain the moment, if you had one, when you unconsciously *knew* you wouldn't marry.

Notes

❈ ❈ ❈

CHAPTER TWO

1. Markman, H. J., Stanley, S. M., and Blumberg, S. L. *Fighting* for *Your Marriage: Positive Steps for Preventing Divorce and Preserving a Lasting Love.* San Francisco: Jossey-Bass, 2001.
2. Mellan, O. *Money Harmony: Resolving Money Conflicts in Your Life and Relationships.* New York: Walker, 1995. Hayden, R. L. *For Richer, Not Poorer* [http://www.ruthhayden.com/richer_excerpts.html].
3. Michael, R. T., Gagnon, J. H., and Lauman, E. O. *Sex in America: A Definitive Survey.* Boston: Little, Brown, 1994, p. 124.

4. Weston, L. P. *MSNBC Money Central.* [http://moneycentral.msn.com/articles/family/basics/9618.asp]. May 9, 2002.
5. *Blender* magazine.
6. Fowers, B. J., Montel, K. H., and Olson, D. H. *Predicting Marital Success for Premarital Couple Types Based on PREPARE.* 1996.
7. Harley, W. F. *His Needs, Her Needs: Building an Affair-Proof Marriage.* (15th anniv. ed.) Grand Rapids, Mich.: Revell, 2001.
8. Fowers, Montel, and Olson, 1996.
9. Copyright FOCCUS, Inc., Omaha, Nebraska, 1985, 1997, 2000. No reprinting or photocopying without permission. Statements are taken from FOCCUS, Facilitating Open Couple Communication, Understanding and Study.

CHAPTER FOUR

1. Martin, J. *Miss Manners on Weddings.* New York: Crown, 1999. (Previously published as *Miss Manners on Painfully Proper Weddings.* New York: Crown, 1996.)

CHAPTER FIVE

1. Martin, 1999.
2. Tushnet, R. "Rules of Engagement." *Yale Law Journal,* June 1998. Originally Zabito, T. "Man Sues Ex-Fiancée to Get Ring Back: What Do Advice Columnists Say?" *Record* (N.J.), Aug. 28, 1996, p. N1.
3. Hax, C., personal communication with author, Nov. 2002.
4. Tushnet, June 1998. Originally Zabito, Aug. 28, 1996.

5. Tushnet, June 1998. Originally Martin, J., "Finding a Way to Stop Passengers from Taking Control." *Chicago Tribune*, Jan. 25, 1996, p. 11.
6. Dear Prudence. [http://slate.msn.com/?id=98088]. Feb. 1, 2001.
7. Dear Prudence. [http://slate.msn.com/?id=2060181]. Jan. 3, 2002.
8. Tushnet, R. Originally Piccininni v. Hajus (1980), 180 Conn. 369, 429 A.2d 886, 888. (Quoted from Vann v. Vehrs, Appellate Court of Illinois, Second District. 260 Ill. App. 3d 648; 633 N.E. 2d 102; 1994 Ill. App. LEXIS 562; 198 Ill. Dec. 640, Dec. 20, 1993. Submitted Apr. 19, 1994, Filed.)
9. Tushnet, R. "Rules of Engagement." Originally Brockelbank, W. J. "The Nature of a Promise to Marry: A Study in Comparative Law" (pt. 2), 41 Ill. L. Rev. 199, pp. 207–208 (1946).
10. Tushnet, R. "Rules of Engagement." Originally Pavlicic v. Vogtsberger, 136 A. 2d, 1957, pp. 130–131.
11. Tushnet, R. "Rules of Engagement." Originally Pavlicic v. Vogtsberger, 136 A. 2d, 1957.
12. Tushnet, R. "Rules of Engagement." Originally Wright, H. F. *Note, the Action for Breach of Marriage Promise,* 10 Va. L. Rev. 361 (1924), p. 377.
13. Grossman, J. L. "Who Gets the Engagement Ring When the Wedding Is Off?" Oct. 23, 2001. http://writ.news.findlaw.com/grossman/20011023.html.
14. Tushnet, R. "Rules of Engagement." Originally Harris v. Davis, Illinois Appellate Court, 1968.
15. Tushnet, R. "Rules of Engagement," June, 1998.
16. Gill v. Shively, 320 So. 2d 415 Fla., 4th DCA, 1975, p. 484.
17. Monchek-Lugo, B., personal communication with author, Aug. 2002.
18. Grossman, Oct. 23, 2001.

19. Tushnet, R. "Rules of Engagement," June 1998.
20. Tushnet, R., personal communication with author, Aug. 2002.
21. Grossman, Oct. 23, 2001.
22. Tushnet, R., personal communication with author, Aug. 2002.

CHAPTER SIX

1. Woolf, V. *A Room of One's Own.* New York: Harcourt, 1957, p. 38. (Originally published 1929.)
2. de Beauvoir, S. *The Second Sex.* New York: Vintage, 1989, p. 137. (Originally published 1952.)
3. Steinem, G. "I Was a Playboy Bunny." In G. Steinem, *Outrageous Acts and Everyday Rebellions.* New York: Henry Holt, 1995. Originally published in *Show* magazine, 1963.
4. Faludi, S. *Backlash: The Undeclared War Against American Women.* New York: Anchor Books, 1992, p. 16.
5. Yalom, M. *A History of the Wife.* New York: HarperCollins, 2001, p. xii.
6. Geller, J. *Here Comes the Bride: Women, Weddings and the Marriage Mystique.* New York: Four Walls Eight Windows, 2001, p. 72.
7. Greer, G. *The Whole Woman.* New York: Anchor Books, 2000, p. 256.
8. Fein, E., and Schneider, S. *The Rules: Time-Tested Secrets for Capturing the Heart of Mr. Right.* New York: Warner Books, 1995.
9. Orenstein, P. *Flux: Women on Sex, Work, Love, Kids, and Life in a Half-Changed World.* New York: Doubleday, 2000, p. 284.
10. Orenstein, P., 2000, p. 233.

11. Friedan, B. *The Feminine Mystique.* New York: Norton, 1983, p. 74. (Originally published 1963.)

12. For more information on Emma Goldman, see http://sunsite.berkeley.edu/Goldman.

13. Goldman, E. "Marriage and Love." In M. Schneir (ed.), *Feminism: The Essential Historical Writings.* New York: Vintage Books, 1972, 1992. Originally in Goldman, E., *Anarchism and Other Essays.* New York: Associated Faculty Press, 1911. Also found in Goldman, E. *Red Emma Speaks: Selected Writings and Speeches of Emma Goldman.* (Edited by Alix Kates Shulman.) New York: Random House, 1972.

14. Faludi, 1992, p. 14.

15. Orenstein, 2000, p. 241.

16. Wallerstein, J., and Blakeslee, S. *The Good Marriage: How and Why Love Lasts.* Boston: Houghton Mifflin, 1995, p. 5.

17. Geller, 2001.

18. Swallow, W. *Breaking Apart.* New York: Hyperion Books, 2000.

19. Swallow, W. "The Case for Getting Married Again, or, the Reluctant Bride." *Washingtonian* magazine, Feb. 2002.

20. Harris, L. *Rules of Engagement: Four Couples and the American Marriage Today.* New York: Simon & Schuster, 1996, p. 42.

21. Copeland, L. "The State of the Union? Pretty Short, for Starters." *The Washington Post,* Jan. 31, 2002.

22. Dewan, S. K. "No Dress, No Vows, and Less Status in Grief." *The New York Times,* Jan. 22, 2002.

23. Orenstein, 2000, p. 241.

24. Willis, E. "The Last Unmarried Person in America." Excerpted from *No More Nice Girls: Countercultural Essays.* Middletown, Conn.: Wesleyan University Press, 1993.

25. Tiger, L. "Omnigamy: A New Kingship System." In M. Stubbs and S. Bennett (eds.), *The Little, Brown Reader.* Boston: Little, Brown, 1986, p. 20.
26. Geller, 2001, p. 327.
27. Heyn, D. *Marriage Shock: The Transformation of Women into Wives.* New York: Villard Books, 1997, p. 17.
28. Heyn, 1997, p. 17.
29. Heyn, 1997, pp. 132–133.
30. Heyn, 1997, p. 191.
31. "Trial Runs." *People Magazine,* Mar. 25, 2002.

CHAPTER SEVEN

1. Roth, M. *On the Loose: Big-City Days and Nights of Three Single Women.* New York: Morrow, 1999.
2. Schwartz, J. *Macaroni and Cheese: 52 Recipes from the Simple to the Sublime.* New York: Villard Books, 2001.
3. Gray, J. *Mars and Venus Starting Over.* New York: HarperCollins, 1998, p. 179.

CHAPTER EIGHT

1. Moody, R., Jr., and Arcangel, D. *Life After Loss: Conquering Grief and Finding Hope.* San Francisco: HarperSanFrancisco, 2001, pp. 36–37.
2. Moody and Arcangel, 2001, p. 37.
3. Moody and Arcangel, 2001, p. 38.
4. Kübler-Ross, E. *On Death and Dying.* New York: Collier Books, and Old Tappan, N.J.: MacMillan, 1969.
5. Kübler-Ross, 1969, p. 100.
6. Kübler-Ross, 1969, pp. 123–124.
7. Kübler-Ross, 1969, pp. 123–124.

8. Freud, S. *Mourning and Melancholia: Standard Edition of The Complete Psychological Works of Sigmund Freud, SE 14.* London: Hogarth Press Limited, 1917.
9. Moody and Arcangel, 2001, pp. 10–11.
10. Moody and Arcangel, 2001, pp. 40–41.
11. Moody and Arcangel, 2001, pp. 41–43.
12. Moody and Arcangel, 2001, pp. 10–11.
13. Moody and Arcangel, 2001, pp. 46–47.
14. Moody and Arcangel, 2001, p. 48.
15. Moody and Arcangel, 2001, p. 49.

WORKS CONSULTED FOR CHAPTER EIGHT

Bowlby, J. *Attachment and Loss, Volume II: Separation, Anxiety and Anger.* New York: Basic Books, 1973.

Bowlby, J. *Attachment and Loss, Volume III: Loss, Sadness and Depression.* New York: Basic Books, 1980.

Deits, B. *Life After Loss: A Personal Guide to Dealing with Death, Divorce, Job Change and Relocation.* (3rd ed.) Cambridge, Mass.: Fisher Books, 1988.

James, J. W., and Friedman, R. *The Grief Recovery Handbook: The Action Program for Moving Beyond Death, Divorce and Other Losses.* (Rev. ed.) New York: HarperPerennial, 1998.

CHAPTER NINE

1. *Depression,* NIH publication No. 00–3561. Printed in 2000. [Available at http://www.nimh.nih.gov/publicat/depression.cfm#ptdep3].
2. *Diagnostic and Statistical Manual of Mental Disorders* (DSM-IV-TR, text version). (4th ed.) New York: McGraw-Hill/Contemporary Books, 1994, 2001,

p. 345. Turkington, C., and Kaplan, E. F. *Making the Anti-Depressant Decision: How to Choose the Right Treatment Option for You or Your Loved One.* (3rd. ed.) New York: McGraw-Hill/Contemporary Books, 2001, p. 7.

3. *Diagnostic and Statistic Manual for Mental Disorders,* 2001, pp. 339–344.

4. *Diagnostic and Statistical Manual for Mental Disorders,* 2001, p. 345.

5. *Diagnostic and Statistical Manual for Mental Disorders,* 2001, pp. 345–349.

6. *Diagnostic and Statistical Manual for Mental Disorders,* 2001, pp. 623–627.

7. *Diagnostic and Statistical Manual for Mental Disorders,* 2001, p. 340.

8. Turkington and Kaplan, 2001, pp. 5–6, 32.

9. Raskin, V. D. *When Words Are Not Enough: The Woman's Prescription for Depression and Anxiety.* New York: Broadway Books, 1997, p. 253.

10. Turkington and Kaplan, 2001, pp. 54–58.

The Authors

❋ ❋ ❋

Rachel Safier has written for magazines, television, and the Web. Her diverse portfolio includes a write-up of a Vanilla Ice concert for *Seventeen* magazine, reviews of feminist works for *Publishers Weekly,* reports on vacation spots in *U.S. News & World Report*'s annual travel guide, and myriad vignettes for Bloomberg News, on everything from dieting to peace in the Middle East, all delivered by former New York mayor Ed Koch. She and her fiancé broke their engagement two weeks before their scheduled wedding day. She is the founder of the Web site theregoesthebride.com.

Licensed clinical social worker Wendy Roberts has been in private practice for nearly twenty-five years. Her practice in Falls Church, Virginia, deals with individuals, couples, and family psychotherapy, and her experience includes individual and group therapy with female adolescents at the Karma Academy for Girls in Rockville, Maryland.

ANOTHER BOOK OF INTEREST

Including Self-Tests from the RELATE Premarital Questionnaire — Jeffry H. Larson, Ph.D.

Should We Stay Together?

A SCIENTIFICALLY PROVEN METHOD FOR EVALUATING YOUR RELATIONSHIP AND IMPROVING ITS CHANCES FOR LONG-TERM SUCCESS

Should We Stay Together? A Scientifically Proven Method for Evaluating Your Relationship and Improving Its Chances for Long-Term Success

Jeffry H. Larson, Ph.D.

$25.00 Paper

ISBN: 0-7879-5144-7

"Here's your chance to learn more about the potential of your relationship. With this book, you'll learn about the things that put marriages—maybe yours—at risk and, more importantly, what areas you need to focus on to build a lasting and happy relationship. With its strong basis in marital research, I highly recommend this book for those wanting to make a solid investment in their future together."

—**Scott M. Stanley**, coauthor, *Fighting for Your Marriage*

W ill we live happily ever after?

The fact is that some couples need more time to mature, some need to work through specific issues, and some should never be together. But how do you know? What factors add up to success or failure in a relationship? Author Jeffry Larson knows. In fact, he knows a lot about what predicts a happy marriage. Based on Larson's twenty-plus years of research and experience in marriage and family therapy, *Should We Stay Together?* debunks many time-honored myths as it provides couples with the tools they need to make better decisions and thoroughly explore every aspect of their relationship. From individual characteristics, idiosyncratic family histories, unresolved conflicts and needs, and combined strengths and weaknesses, this step-by-step scientific method for relationship evaluation—based on the highly accurate RELATE premarital assessment questionnaire—will help couples understand the specific traits that predict a satisfying or disastrous relationship.

JEFFRY H. LARSON, Ph.D., is chairperson, Department of Marriage and Family Therapy, Brigham Young University. He was chairperson of the Marriage Preparation Focus Group of the National Council on Family Relations and has been a marriage and family therapist for more than twenty-two years. He is the author of *The Great Marriage Tune-Up Book*.

[Price subject to change]